# GodChick Devo
# Putting Down Roots

A 52-week devotional that encourages you to see God in the ordinary and build a solid foundation in His word

Written By: Allison T. Cain

They will be like a tree planted by the water that sends out its **roots** by the stream. It does not fear when heat comes; its leaves are always green. It has no worries in a year of drought and never fails to bear fruit."

Jeremiah 17:8

GodChick Devotions: Putting Down Roots

Editor – Jeannie Norris

Published 2011. All rights reserved.
Copyright © 2011 by Allison T. Cain
No portion of this book, either art work, photographs, design or text may be reproduced in any form without written permission from Allison T. Cain, except for brief quotations used in reviews.

Unless otherwise noted, scripture quotations are from the Holy Bible, New International Version, copyright © 1973, 1978, 1984 by International Bible Society.

Scripture taken from The Message. copyright © 1993, 1994, 1995, 1996, 2000, 2001, 2002. Used by permission of NavPress Publishing Group.

Bing® Online Dictionary was used for all word definitions unless noted.

Allison T. Cain
[atcain2@earthlink.net]

ISBN 9781466315747

FIRST PRINTING

To order additional copies of this resource, visit www.godchickdevotions.com for store locations, www.amazon.com or e-mail atcain2@earthlink.net.

Printed in the United States of America

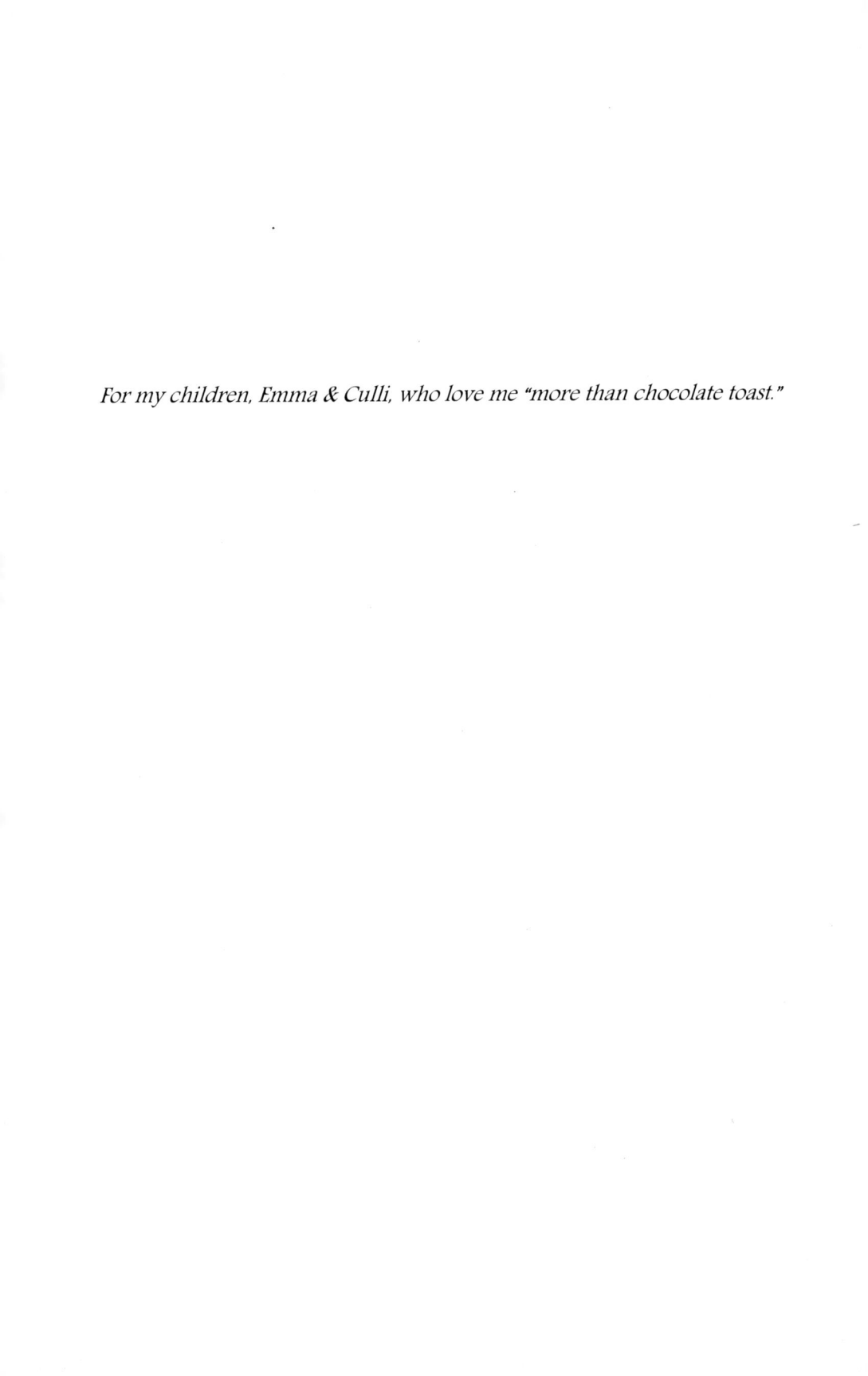

*For my children, Emma & Culli, who love me "more than chocolate toast."*

*GodChick Devotions: Putting Down Roots*
www.godchickdevotions.com

Encouraging ALL women to see God in the ordinary

\*\*\*

## Introduction

In this devotional, I incorporate the skills we practiced in my Bible study, *In the Mi[God]dle*, with reflections from *The Whisper of God* devotional. My prayer is that, through these combined resources, your devotional time will launch you into a deeper relationship with our Father in Heaven and give you a solid foundation in His word.

## How to use this devotional

First things, First!

Before you begin this devotional, pray God opens your mind to His word. He wants to help us and all we have to do is ask.

Look up and write out these verses:

**Jeremiah 33:3**



**Luke 11:9**



**James 1:5**

What are these verses saying? Ask and receive the Holy Spirit's direction before you begin each day. You don't need a long prayer. Just a simple, "Father, please open my heart and mind to Your written Word today so that I may draw closer to You." He wants to help you, and all you have to do it ask.

GodChick Devotions contains 52 devotions, one for each week of the year. After each devotion, is a section for you to write your thoughts and revelations. You may need more space, so I encourage you to pick up one of those empty journals (if you are like me) and start filling it up. Or you visit my website (**www.godchickdevotions.com**) to print off worksheets under the "continued study" section.

### Monday- Find a Word

Choose a word from the devotion or cited scriptures to reflect on for the week. Some examples: sovereign, righteous, almighty, full, uphold, future, hope, love, obedience

Use your Bible index/reference or search your favorite online Bible the scriptures containing the word you chose. Write out at least five of the verses you find. We will go back and read them after we have compiled the list.

Go back to read the five verses and make notes in your journal about each one. Pray God will open your mind to understand His word and your heart will receive a fresh revelation from Him.

As you reflect on the scriptures, ask yourself what you think God wants you to hear.

## Tuesday – Define

Choose one or two words from each Bible verse that you want to look up in the dictionary. Write out the words and their definitions. Then, reread the scriptures and replace each word with its definition. How did it take your scriptural understanding to a new level?

For example:

**Return to the Lord your God, for he is <u>gracious</u> and compassionate, slow to anger and <u>abounding</u> in love, and he <u>relents</u> from sending calamity." Joel 2:13 (emphasis mine)**

**Gracious** – kind, polite, generous
**Abounding** – great in number or amount
**Relents** – to become more sympathetic, to surrender, to give in and become less intense

I don't know about you, but when I reread the scriptures and replace those words with their definitions, I gain new meaning, feeling and understanding that I otherwise may have missed or passed over.

## Wednesday – Translate

Choose two to three different Bible translations and read the Monday verses in each. I like to use the King James, NIV and The Message translations. You may have another favorite. Using an online Bible resource like biblegateway.com will help a lot. Write out the verses in your journal or on another sheet of paper.

## Thursday – Go the Distance

Take one of your favorite verses from the week's devotion and read the entire chapter. For example, if you found Jeremiah 29:11 especially meaningful, go to Jeremiah and read the entire 29th chapter. This will give the verse more context and may open a deeper meaning for you.

## Friday – Prayer

Reflect on the verses you've studied, and through prayer, thank God for all He revealed to you during the week.

Each devotion includes a reminder of what to do, and you can refer back to these examples for the first few weeks until you get into a groove. I pray that through your commitment and study God knocks your socks off!

*All scriptures are cited in bold and in the NIV translation unless otherwise noted.*

# Week 1 ~ The Old Days

Eat honey, dear child – it's good for you – and delicacies that melt in your mouth. Likewise knowledge, and wisdom for your soul – Get that and your future's secured, your hope is on solid rock. Proverbs 24:13 (The Message)

When my youngest started kindergarten, it was not the easiest transition for either of us. He figured out that kindergarten takes him away from me for seven hours instead of pre-kindergarten's three hours. "I just want things to go back to the way they used to be," he said with a tear rolling down his cheek.

**"For I know the plans I have for you," declares the LORD, "plans to prosper you and not to harm you, plans to give you hope and a future." Jeremiah 29:11**

I started thinking of all the people around me going through change and transition and how many of them long for "the old days." The days before commitments were broken, before a tumor was found on a child's brain, before job loss severed their finances, before they gave in to temptation of the flesh . . . before, before, before. I told my son that we have to "keep moving forward." We need to keep our eyes on the Lord because, if we look away for one moment during trying times, the enemy will step in to overtake our hope, strength and perseverance with fear, sadness and despair. Keeping our eyes focused on Him will not stop us from bending under the pressure, but it will guarantee we don't break. Even in the midst of unhappiness, our trials will bring growth and joy in the Lord and lead us into a deeper and closer relationship with Him.

**Consider it pure joy, my brothers and sisters, whenever you face trials of many kinds, because you know that the testing of your faith produces perseverance. James 1: 2-3**

My husband says that we're on track to receive our Ph.D. in overcoming trials and leaning on God's understanding rather than our own. I am thankful God loves and cares enough to guide us through these trials of life. He is the One who gives us courage and strength to face the next day, to overcome the challenge, to keep our eyes on Him and to live for today – not yesterday.

I pray that when we're called to walk across that graduation stage one day, it's with an outstretched hand, and our Father in heaven will look at us and say, "Well done, good and faithful servant." Matthew 25:23

**Let perseverance finish its work so that you may be mature and complete, not lacking anything. James 1:4**

~~~~~~

### Monday – Find a word
Choose a word from the devotion or cited scriptures to reflect on for the week. Some examples: sovereign, righteous, almighty, full, uphold, future, hope, love, obedience.

What is your word? _____

Search your Bible commentary. What verses use your word? List them here. Use your journal if you need additional space.

_____
_____
_____

### Tuesday – Define
Choose one to two words to define and then reread the scriptures, replacing the word with the definition. How did it take your understanding to a new level?

### Wednesday – Translate
Choose two or three different Bible translations. Read the Monday verses (cited in the devotional or found in your study) in each translation. Now write them in your journal.

### Thursday – Go the Distance
Read the entire chapter of your favorite verse for the week.

### Friday – Prayer
Close your eyes and talk to God or write out your prayer in your journal.

# Week 2 ~ Waves of Life

He is the Rock, his works are perfect, and all his ways are just. A faithful God who does no wrong, upright and just is he. Deuteronomy 32:4

As I enjoyed a quiet walk on the beach, a beautiful shell caught my eye. Just as I reached down to pick it up, a wave rolled in and I knew it had been washed away. But when the wave receded into the ocean, the shell remained and I picked it up. It wasn't perfect or complete. It was really just the remains of a shell – all twists and turns, with edges eroded to soft curves by the power of the surf. It was beautiful to me. I held it in my hand and continued my walk. A few minutes later another shell caught my eye. This one was different. It was complete, perfect and shiny. It looked almost like a piece of glass. Again, as I stooped to pick it up a wave rolled in, but this time the shell was gone when the water receded.

**Don't look for shortcuts to God. The market is flooded with surefire, easygoing formulas for a successful life that can be practiced in your spare time. Don't fall for that stuff, even though crowds of people do. The way to life – to God! – is vigorous and requires total attention. Matthew 7:13 (The Message)**

Like many people, I feel very close to God when I'm on the water – especially at the beach. As I was walking, my mind was on Him and, of course as the GodChick, I saw His lesson for me in these two shells. It was a tangible way of reminding me that life always takes twists and turns. There will be many things I endure, but He will use them to make me beautiful in my own way – in HIS way. And unlike the shiny things of this world that compete endlessly for my attention, He alone is my "everlasting to everlasting." All worldly things will melt away. They are here only for an instant, but He lasts an eternity.

**"Stand up and praise the LORD your God, who is from everlasting to everlasting." "Blessed be your glorious name, and may it be exalted above all blessing and praise." Nehemiah 9:5**

God is all around, teaching us through His word, through our lives and those near us, and in our conversations with Him. I pray as you follow these devotions, you are beginning to notice God more in your everyday life.

~~~~~~

### Monday – Find a word

Choose a word from the devotion or cited scriptures to reflect on for the week. Some examples: sovereign, righteous, almighty, full, uphold, future, hope, love, obedience.

What is your word? _____

Search your Bible commentary. What verses use your word? List them here. Use your journal if you need additional space.

_____
_____
_____
_____

### Tuesday – Define

Choose one to two words to define and then reread the scriptures, replacing the word with the definition. How did it take your understanding to a new level?

### Wednesday – Translate

Choose two or three different Bible translations. Read the Monday verses (cited in the devotional or found in your study) in each translation. Now write them in your journal.

### Thursday – Go the Distance

Read the entire chapter of your favorite verse for the week.

### Friday – Prayer

Close your eyes and talk to God or write out your prayer in your journal.

# Week 3 ~ Warped

You have heard that it was said, "Eye for eye, and tooth for tooth." But I tell you, do not resist an evil person. If anyone slaps you on the right cheek, turn to them the other cheek also. And if anyone wants to sue you and take your shirt, hand over your coat as well. If anyone forces you to go one mile, go with them two miles. Give to the one who asks you, and do not turn away from the one who wants to borrow from you. Matthew 5:38-42

After pushing his sister, my son defended himself with a really warped statement. He said, "Well, Mommy, God always says treat others the way you want to be treated. She pushed me first, so I guess she wanted me to push her." I am sure you can imagine the look on my face as those words came out of his mouth. "Whoa!" I declared before sending him to his room to think about things. "You are responsible for your actions – not the actions of others. God also says turn the other cheek."

My son's statement reminded me how we take God's word and twist it to our liking. We twist His laws for our own purposes – to defend or excuse our own actions. We warp His holy word and we fail to take the time to know it for ourselves. Some of us actually believe the Bible includes statements like "cleanliness is next to godliness," "money is the root of all evil" and "God helps those who help themselves." We believe mistruths because we listen to what others tell us the Bible says rather than spending the time to read it ourselves. We must invest our time and hearts fully in knowing God. This is an important part of my ministry; I want to encourage all women to see God in the ordinary, to seek Him and know Him on a personal and intimate level by diving into His word. If you are trying to find another way, it will lead you to a dead end.

When people tell you, "Try out the fortunetellers. Consult the spiritualists. Why not tap into the spirit-world, get in touch with the dead?" Tell them, "No, we're going to study the Scriptures." People who try the other ways get nowhere – a dead end! Frustrated and famished, they try one thing after another. When nothing works out they get angry, cursing first this god and then that one,

Looking this way and that, up, down, and sideways – and seeing nothing, A blank wall, an empty hole. They end up in the dark with nothing. Isaiah 8:19 (The Message)

In Deuteronomy 22, He says that even if you see a wandering or injured sheep or ox, don't look the other way. Return it. God desires for us to care for and show compassion to the sheep and oxen – how much more does He want us to show compassion for our neighbor and brother or sister in Christ? In short, we must treat them the way we would like to be treated. Taking time to read and understand God's word fills us with the knowledge we need to go out into this world and do just that.

~~~~~~

### Monday – Find a word
Choose a word from the devotion or cited scriptures to reflect on for the week. Some examples: sovereign, righteous, almighty, full, uphold, future, hope, love, obedience.

What is your word? _____

Search your Bible commentary. What verses use your word? List them here. Use your journal if you need additional space.

_____
_____
_____

### Tuesday – Define
Choose one to two words to define and then reread the scriptures, replacing the word with the definition. How did it take your understanding to a new level?

### Wednesday – Translate
Choose two or three different Bible translations. Read the Monday verses (cited in the devotional or found in your study) in each translation. Now write them in your journal.

### Thursday – Go the Distance
Read the entire chapter of your favorite verse for the week.

### Friday – Prayer
Close your eyes and talk to God or write out your prayer in your journal.

# Week 4 ~ Sound The Alarm

One morning, as my husband and I got ready for the day, the kids were busy running in and out of the house. I keep the chime feature activated on our alarm system so that I'm alerted when a door opens. This particular morning the "alarm lady" was very busy, saying "sliding door" in her calm, beautiful British accent every few minutes. I don't know what the kids were doing, but they were going in and out the door so frequently that it became a joke. My husband said, "Do you think she ever gets tired of saying that?" "No," I responded. "She never even gets angry or raises her voice."

**Therefore, as God's chosen people, holy and dearly loved, clothe yourselves with compassion, kindness, humility, gentleness and patience. Colossians 1:11**

**And he passed in front of Moses, proclaiming, "The LORD, the LORD, the compassionate and gracious God, slow to anger, abounding in love and faithfulness, Exodus 34:6**

**The LORD is gracious and compassionate, slow to anger and rich in love. Psalm 145:8**

Praise the Lord we have a patient God. Let's be honest – if He wasn't, we would all be in a heap of trouble. I have days when I struggle with worldly desires. I have to ask for forgiveness and hand over my weakness to Him multiple times – sometimes hourly! I am sure God feels like the "alarm lady" sometimes. When I open the door to sin and then ask for forgiveness, He replies, "You are forgiven." I am so thankful He never grows weary of my desire to come to Him and seek Him for forgiveness. I use His power and courage to get out there and do a better job next time.

Like the child who knows how to manipulate his parents and talk them out of punishment, we must be careful not to take God's patience, grace and forgiveness for granted. God is "great in power" and holds us accountable for our actions! Notice the Bible says, "He is slow to anger." It does not say He never gets angry.

The old saying about asking forgiveness rather than permission doesn't get us far when we're trying to lead a Christian life. If we truly believe in Jesus and the word of God, our hearts and minds begin to change in ways we could never imagine. Please understand, though, I am not saying that once we believe in God we'll never sin again or be tempted by sin or mess up BIG TIME. We are human, after all, and always have that potential. What I'm saying is that when we seek God with an earnest plea for forgiveness, He will forgive; but when we use His forgiveness as an excuse to sin, it's time to sound the alarm and check our hearts.

**The LORD is slow to anger but great in power; the LORD will not leave the guilty unpunished. His way is in the whirlwind and the storm, and clouds are the dust of his feet. Nahum 1:3**

~~~~~~

### Monday – Find a word
Choose a word from the devotion or cited scriptures to reflect on for the week. Some examples: sovereign, righteous, almighty, full, uphold, future, hope, love, obedience.
What is your word? _____
Search your Bible commentary. What verses use your word? List them here. Use your journal if you need additional space.
_____
_____
_____

### Tuesday – Define
Choose one to two words to define and then reread the scriptures, replacing the word with the definition. How did it take your understanding to a new level?

### Wednesday – Translate
Choose two or three different Bible translations. Read the Monday verses (cited in the devotional or found in your study) in each translation. Now write them in your journal.

### Thursday – Go the Distance
Read the entire chapter of your favorite verse for the week.

### Friday – Prayer
Close your eyes and talk to God or write out your prayer in your journal.

# Week 5 ~ Ezra

Those who stay behind, wherever they happen to live, will support them with silver, gold, tools, and pack animals, along with Freewill-Offerings for The Temple of God in Jerusalem. The heads of the families of Judah and Benjamin, along with the priests and Levites – everyone, in fact, God prodded – set out to build The Temple of God in Jerusalem. Their neighbors rallied behind them enthusiastically with silver, gold, tools, pack animals, expensive gifts, and, over and above these, Freewill-Offerings. Ezra 1:2-6 (The Message)

I had never studied the book of Ezra in great detail – or much at all – until recently. It was the first chapter, second through sixth verses, that caught my eye right away. A little history is needed to really understand the importance of these passages. The Israelites had been captured and displaced to the "sin city" of Babylon for years before Cyrus came into power and issued a decree allowing them to return to their sacred homeland. Displacing these people would be like taking a monk out of a monastery and relocating him to Las Vegas. But many Israelites had become successful during those years of captivity and had grown accustomed to their new lifestyle. When given the opportunity to return to Jerusalem, "the number of the exiles that chose to remain was probably about six times the number of those who returned." (Eastman's Bible Dictionary) This dynamic created two groups of Israelites. The first group chose to stay in Babylon but gave generously to those returning home for the construction of a temple. The second group was thrilled to return home after all those years of captivity and would not have stayed in Babylon another moment. Each made a choice, and there was no judgment from either side. Read the verses again. Did you notice? There was no judgment from either side. Only generosity, grace and joy. Each group seemed thrilled for the other even though they had chosen different paths. Maybe Ezra left out the backstabbing and judgment part of the story or maybe it really went down without any drama.

I have not been able to get those first verses off my mind. Unfortunately, it seems more reasonable (when dealing with people) that Ezra left out part of the story. There is no way the Isrealites' return could have gone that smoothly, right?

But what if it did? What if their firm foundation in God never left during captivity and kept their hearts in check? Only God's love, grace and kindness could penetrate a human heart enough to produce that kind of effect in people. Only God's promises and peace can produce results that amazing in such an overwhelming situation.

I don't know about you, but I pray God will bring these verses to mind when I am in situations that seem unfair or I am quick to judge. We are not capable of the patience, love and grace we need to bestow on those around us, but God is capable! Let Him handle it. We are all a part of the body of Christ, and each part is called to something different than the other. God calls us to honor those differences.

~~~~~~

### Monday – Find a word
Choose a word from the devotion or cited scriptures to reflect on for the week. Some examples: sovereign, righteous, almighty, full, uphold, future, hope, love, obedience. What is your word? _____
Search your Bible commentary. What verses use your word? List them here. Use your journal if you need additional space.

_____
_____
_____
_____

### Tuesday – Define
Choose one to two words to define and then reread the scriptures, replacing the word with the definition. How did it take your understanding to a new level?

### Wednesday – Translate
Choose two or three different Bible translations. Read the Monday verses (cited in the devotional or found in your study) in each translation. Now write them in your journal.

### Thursday – Go the Distance
Read the entire chapter of your favorite verse for the week.

### Friday – Prayer
Close your eyes and talk to God or write out your prayer in your journal.

# Week 6 ~ Back Against the Wall

You know the moments when turning your life over to God is the only option you have, because if He doesn't show up your goose is totally cooked? We shouldn't even try to take control of the situation – we should take it straight to God in prayer because it is completely out of our hands.

It would be nice if we instantly handed EVERYTHING over to God, ALL the time. But we are human. As humans, it's our nature to try to control circumstances so they work out according to our own plans. We want to trust, but we hold onto things believing that God doesn't care about the small stuff or we can handle it better and faster. Oh, how many times I've gotten into trouble in my life by trusting this illusion of control. I always feel better when I see my flaws in the people of the Bible. As I continued to study Ezra, I saw how he fell prey to this lack of trust. It was time for Ezra to return to his homeland, so he gathered up a great group of men. They had a long and difficult journey ahead of them.

**I proclaimed a fast there beside the Ahava Canal, a fast to humble ourselves before our God and pray for wise guidance for our journey – all our people and possessions. I was embarrassed to ask the king for a cavalry bodyguard to protect us from bandits on the road. We had just told the king, "Our God lovingly looks after all those who seek him, but turns away in disgust from those who leave him." So we fasted and prayed about these concerns. And he listened. Ezra 8:21-23 (The Message)**

Did you catch it? It's amazing that just a couple of verses can hold such great meaning! Here is Ezra, proclaiming that God protects and looks after those who seek Him, but fearing at the same time the dangers that lie ahead on his long journey. Does this sound familiar? He was too embarrassed to ask the king for help after all His proclamations about our good and faithful God. Ezra had no other option than to turn to fasting and prayer while hoping that God answered. Verse 23 tells us, "He (God) listened." Ezra shares our human weaknesses. We say we trust our loving Father. We say He protects and shields those who seek Him. We say we love Him above all else. Do we only say those words or do we live them? Do we believe them only when there is nothing left for us to control?

I am not going to sugarcoat this point. We will struggle the rest of our days with Satan's deception that we are in control. I pray God opens our eyes to this deception and continues to tug at our hearts so we draw closer to Him and rest in Him more fervently every day. TRUST in Him!

~~~~~~

### Monday – Find a word

Choose a word from the devotion or cited scriptures to reflect on for the week. Some examples: sovereign, righteous, almighty, full, uphold, future, hope, love, obedience.

What is your word? _____

Search your Bible commentary. What verses use your word? List them here. Use your journal if you need additional space.

_____
_____
_____
_____

### Tuesday – Define

Choose one to two words to define and then reread the scriptures, replacing the word with the definition. How did it take your understanding to a new level?

### Wednesday – Translate

Choose two or three different Bible translations. Read the Monday verses (cited in the devotional or found in your study) in each translation. Now write them in your journal.

### Thursday – Go the Distance

Read the entire chapter of your favorite verse for the week.

### Friday – Prayer

Close your eyes and talk to God or write out your prayer in your journal.

# Week 7 ~ A Grip on Hope

Lately it's seemed that every time I talk to a friend, receive an e-mail or prayer request, or see the news, there's another story of death, despair and heartache. It is overwhelming. In fact, when I think about friends facing a child's terminal illness, a loved one's imprisonment or the financial pressures of job loss, I wonder how they bear it. So when I read Lamentations 3 (The Message), the first three verses hit hard. Jeremiah is feeling God had abandoned him and the nation of Judah.

**I'm the man who has seen trouble, trouble coming from the lash of God's anger. He took me by the hand and walked me into pitch-black darkness. Yes, he's given me the back of his hand over and over and over again. Lamentations 3:1-3**

It doesn't stop there. Jeremiah continues and says, **Even when I cry out and plead for help, he locks up my prayers and throws away the key (v. 8), He's a prowling bear tracking me down, a lion in hiding ready to pounce, He knocked me from the path and ripped me to pieces. When he finished, there was nothing left of me (v. 10-11).** And finally he says, **"He ground my face into the gravel. He pounded me into the mud. I gave up on life altogether. I've forgotten what the good life is like. I said to myself, "This is it. I'm finished. God is a lost cause." (v.16-18)**

Have you ever felt like crying out to the Lord with some of these same thoughts or feelings? Have you felt like you finally got your footing, just crawled (or clawed) up from your knees and took a breath only to be knocked down by another blow? I have been there and if you have, too, you are not alone. So what is the good news?

Now read verses 10-35 slowly and soak in every word. I put a few here to get you started. Even in the darkness . . . .

**I'll never forget the trouble, the utter lostness,**
**the taste of ashes, the poison I've swallowed.**
**I remember it all – oh, how well I remember –**
**the feeling of hitting the bottom. (v. 19-21)**

There are some amazing truths in these verses: Keep a grip on hope, God's love and mercy never run out, His mercies are new every morning, pray, wait for hope and the Master never leaves our side. What other truths and characteristics of God stood out? I encourage you to read Lamentations 3 in its entirety and pray God reveals something new to your heart and soothes your soul with the healing balm of His word.

~~~~~~

### Monday – Find a word

Choose a word from the devotion or cited scriptures to reflect on for the week. Some examples: sovereign, righteous, almighty, full, uphold, future, hope, love, obedience. What is your word? _____

Search your Bible commentary. What verses use your word? List them here. Use your journal if you need additional space.

_____
_____
_____
_____

### Tuesday – Define

Choose one to two words to define and then reread the scriptures, replacing the word with the definition. How did it take your understanding to a new level?

### Wednesday – Translate

Choose two or three different Bible translations. Read the Monday verses (cited in the devotional or found in your study) in each translation. Now write them in your journal.

### Thursday – Go the Distance

Read the entire chapter of your favorite verse for the week.

### Friday – Prayer

Close your eyes and talk to God or write out your prayer in your journal.

## Week 8 ~ Hidden

Our children came home from camp and shared all the songs they'd learned there. One of their favorites was "Dynamite." It's a catchy song with fun lyrics, but not one we've listened to before. I usually play contemporary Christian music for them, and I figure I'll do it as long as I can get away with it. Those of you who are parents know what I mean! The world is tugging every day.

One day, as we got into the car with the windows down, they requested their new favorite song. As my husband played it for them, our daughter told her brother, "Quick! Roll up the windows. This is not a Christian song."

**Do you want to stand out? Then step down. Be a servant. If you puff yourself up, you'll get the wind knocked out of you. But if you're content to simply be yourself, your life will count for plenty. Matthew 23:11 (The Message)**

I was convicted as I thought about her statement and all the things we try to hide from others (and ourselves). Whether it's an addiction, a "worldly" idol, an impure thought, a bad habit or lack of faith, we all have something we'd like to hide. The paradox is that the One we try to hide from and the One who loves us most is the One from whom we can never hide. He knows our hearts and minds better than we know ourselves.

**If we had forgotten to pray to our God or made fools of ourselves with store-bought gods, wouldn't God have figured this out? We can't hide things from him. No, you decided to make us martyrs, lambs assigned for sacrifice each day. Psalm 44:20 (The Message)**

What if we redirected all the energy it takes to hide from God and others and put it toward becoming a better disciple? What if we allowed God's strength and power to reign in us? What if we dwelled on His word daily so we had His direction and peace? What if we chose not to hide from Him but allowed Him to protect and hide us from our enemies and the evil of this world?

God has plans to "prosper us not to harm us." **(Jeremiah 29:11)** His plans are "immeasurably more than we could ever imagine." **(Ephesians 3:20)**

I pray we are able to stop hiding and place it all on God's altar so we don't miss out on the plans He had for us before we were created. God will help us overcome our strongholds if we allow Him to help. If we are unable to do so, our full potential is at risk.

**God is bedrock under my feet, the castle in which I live, my rescuing knight. My God – the high crag where I run for dear life, hiding behind the boulders, safe in the granite hideout; My mountaintop refuge, he saves me from ruthless men. 2 Samuel 22:2 (The Message)**

~~~~~~

### Monday – Find a word
Choose a word from the devotion or cited scriptures to reflect on for the week. Some examples: sovereign, righteous, almighty, full, uphold, future, hope, love, obedience. What is your word? _____

Search your Bible commentary. What verses use your word? List them here. Use your journal if you need additional space.

_____
_____
_____
_____


### Tuesday – Define
Choose one to two words to define and then reread the scriptures, replacing the word with the definition. How did it take your understanding to a new level?

### Wednesday – Translate
Choose two or three different Bible translations. Read the Monday verses (cited in the devotional or found in your study) in each translation. Now write them in your journal.

### Thursday – Go the Distance
Read the entire chapter of your favorite verse for the week.

### Friday – Prayer
Close your eyes and talk to God or write out your prayer in your journal.

## Week 9 ~ Seriously

This summer, my daughter joined the swim team for the first time. I hadn't been ready to make the commitment prior to this season and, less than a month into it, I began to wonder what I was thinking when we joined. After the orientation, I visited a friend whose son had been on the team for several years. I told her about a cutting look I'd gotten in the meeting when I'd asked a question, and she told me that many of the parents take swim team "VERY seriously." I said, "I don't take anything that seriously except for Jesus!"

I was convicted when I thought more about my statement. Do I really take Jesus seriously every day? Do I live every minute dying to self – releasing willful, selfish, sinful desires – and letting Him guide my thoughts and ways? One of my greatest fears is becoming a false disciple. Many of us have read and even studied the book of Matthew. I have probably read Matthew 7:21-27 over a dozen times, but God recently opened my eyes and heart to the importance of these verses when I read it in The Message translation.

Matthew 7:21-27 – The Message translation

Knowing the correct password – saying "Master, Master," for instance – isn't going to get you anywhere with me. What is required is serious obedience – doing what my Father wills. I can see it now – at the Final Judgment thousands strutting up to me and saying, "Master, we preached the Message, we bashed the demons, our God-sponsored projects had everyone talking." And do you know what I am going to say? "You missed the boat. All you did was use me to make yourselves important. You don't impress me one bit. You're out of here."

These words I speak to you are not incidental additions to your life, homeowner improvements to your standard of living. They are foundational words, words to build a life on. If you work these words into your life, you are like a smart carpenter who built his house on solid rock. Rain poured down, the river flooded, a tornado hit – but nothing moved that house. It was fixed to the rock.

But if you just use my words in Bible studies and don't work them into your life, you are like a stupid carpenter who built his house on the sandy beach. When a storm rolled in and the waves came up, it collapsed like a house of cards.

His are "foundational words, words to build a life on." Let that sink in. I pray we cement these words in our hearts as we live our lives daily for His glory! Let's take Him seriously!

~~~~~~

### Monday – Find a word
Choose a word from the devotion or cited scriptures to reflect on for the week. Some examples: sovereign, righteous, almighty, full, uphold, future, hope, love, obedience. What is your word? _____

Search your Bible commentary. What verses use your word? List them here. Use your journal if you need additional space.

_____
_____
_____
_____

### Tuesday – Define
Choose one to two words to define and then reread the scriptures, replacing the word with the definition. How did it take your understanding to a new level?

### Wednesday – Translate
Choose two or three different Bible translations. Read the Monday verses (cited in the devotional or found in your study) in each translation. Now write them in your journal.

### Thursday – Go the Distance
Read the entire chapter of your favorite verse for the week.

### Friday – Prayer
Close your eyes and talk to God or write out your prayer in your journal.

## Week 10 ~ But, God

I have written before on how the word "but" can drive me nutty. We use "but" as an excuse or a disclaimer to mean that we're accountable only unless this happens, except for when or contrary to what you think. *But* today I want to look at it from another angle. Let's look at "but" not as an excuse, but as a blessing.

When I was studying Romans 5:8, the "but, God" stood out to me. I decided to research more "but, God" references in scripture and found they are everywhere. Synonyms are: however, nevertheless, still, yet. When you read "but, God," replace it with one of these synonyms for emphasis. Let's take a look.

I am a willful, disobedient sinner and will never come close to measuring up. *But God* demonstrates his own love for us in this: While we were still sinners, Christ died for us. Romans 5:8

I put God on a shelf for so long and was scared to return to Him because of what He would think of me. *But* while he was still a long way off, his father saw him and was filled with compassion for him; he ran to his son, threw his arms around him and kissed him. Luke 15:20

I should never be forgiven for past sins. *But* because of his great love for us, God, who is rich in mercy, ... Ephesians 2:4

I feel all alone, like no one cares and everyone has forgotten me. *But God* will never forget the needy; the hope of the afflicted will never perish. Psalm 9:18

Some days I feel like things are too overwhelming and I wonder how I can go on. My flesh and my heart may fail, *but God* is the strength of my heart and my portion forever. Psalm 73:26

I encourage you to search for more of these during your devotional time this week. There are many, many more. I pray these "but, God" scriptures bring you encouragement, strength, courage and peace.

~~~~~~

### Monday – Find a word

Choose a word from the devotion or cited scriptures to reflect on for the week. Some examples: sovereign, righteous, almighty, full, uphold, future, hope, love, obedience.

What is your word? _____

Search your Bible commentary. What verses use your word? List them here. Use your journal if you need additional space.

_____
_____
_____
_____

### Tuesday – Define

Choose one to two words to define and then reread the scriptures, replacing the word with the definition. How did it take your understanding to a new level?

### Wednesday – Translate

Choose two or three different Bible translations. Read the Monday verses (cited in the devotional or found in your study) in each translation. Now write them in your journal.

### Thursday – Go the Distance

Read the entire chapter of your favorite verse for the week.

### Friday – Prayer

Close your eyes and talk to God or write out your prayer in your journal.

# Week 11 ~ Convenience

If you say, "The LORD is my refuge," and you make the Most High your dwelling, no harm will overtake you, no disaster will come near your tent. For he will command his angels concerning you to guard you in all your ways; they will lift you up in their hands, so that you will not strike your foot against a stone. Psalm 91:9-12

We were rushing out the door (shocker), so I asked my son to please put on his flip-flops because we didn't have time to find and tie his shoes. He was not a bit interested in that. "I don't like flip-flops!" he said, to which I replied, "Come on honey, it's summer. Everyone wears flip-flops in the summer."

**Blessed are those whose ways are blameless, who walk according to the law of the LORD. Blessed are those who keep his statutes and seek him with all their heart – they do no wrong but follow his ways. You have laid down precepts that are to be fully obeyed. Psalm 119:1-4**

"Mommy, just because everyone else does it does not mean I should," he said, throwing my own words (he'd heard so often) back at me. I am just as quick to encourage my daughter to practice piano without fussing – because her friend Molly doesn't fuss – as I am to tell my children that just because Billy drinks soda doesn't mean we should. "Just because someone else does it does not make it right," I tell them. Please tell me I am not the only mom guilty of using persuasion when it's convenient.

My point in this "confessions from a mom" is that we often look to God's word, His laws and His power when it's convenient for us. Real, lasting relationships are not built on convenience. Did you have a friend who called only when she couldn't reach anyone else? How did it make you feel? Think of our God, the Creator of all we see and do not see, the Healer, the Comforter, the Great I AM. When I remind myself of the God I serve and all that He is, it is embarrassing and disappointing to think that I have taken His word so casually. Our God is not here for our convenience. He is here as our Prince of Peace, our Protector, our Mighty Fortress. He IS all we need, but not only when it's convenient for us.

You blew with all your might and the sea covered them. They sank like a lead weight in the majestic waters. Who compares with you among gods, O God? Who compares with you in power, in holy majesty, In awesome praises, wonder-working God? Exodus 15:10 (The Message)

~~~~~~

### Monday – Find a word

Choose a word from the devotion or cited scriptures to reflect on for the week. Some examples: sovereign, righteous, almighty, full, uphold, future, hope, love, obedience.

What is your word? _____

Search your Bible commentary. What verses use your word? List them here. Use your journal if you need additional space.

_____
_____
_____
_____

### Tuesday – Define

Choose one to two words to define and then reread the scriptures, replacing the word with the definition. How did it take your understanding to a new level?

### Wednesday – Translate

Choose two or three different Bible translations. Read the Monday verses (cited in the devotional or found in your study) in each translation. Now write them in your journal.

### Thursday – Go the Distance

Read the entire chapter of your favorite verse for the week.

### Friday – Prayer

Close your eyes and talk to God or write out your prayer in your journal.

# Week 12 ~ Admission

**Every good and perfect gift is from above, coming down from the Father of the heavenly lights, who does not change like shifting shadows. James 1:17**

I have to admit, I once got so tired of hearing my children say "Mommy" a hundred times a day that I took an idea from a sweet friend. I had them pick a new name to call me. (I'm not sure I will offer this option when they're teenagers.) So, for an entire day they called me "GodChick" instead of "Mommy." It was wonderful. Instead of hearing my name and ignoring it or becoming frustrated, I would smile when they called out "GodChick" to get my attention or ask a question. It was such a welcome break.

I am thankful our God never changes, never tires and never sleeps. I am thankful He never grows weary of hearing me call out to Him and asking for the same thing over and over – grace, peace, forgiveness, direction. I praise Him for knowing my heart, knowing that I am trying to live as Jesus calls us and understanding my daily struggle with the flesh. I am thankful for the protection He offers if we are dwelling in His word and abiding in Him. I am also thankful that He is all that I need and will never turn His back on me.

There are hundreds of descriptions of who God is, what He provides and what He has promised in the Bible. This week, I have listed a few descriptions that are meaningful to me, along with the corresponding scripture reference. I hope you will find time in your week to look up these verses and read them as a reminder of all He wants to offer you.

Praise God! He is our:

Guide (Psalm 48:14)
Defender (Psalm 68:5)
Giver (James 1:17)
Comforter (II Cor. 1:4)
Fortress (Psalm 18:2; 91:2 )
Foundation (I Cor. 3:11)

Living Water (John 7:38)
Peace (Ephesians 2:14)
Perfecter (Hebrews 12:2)
Physician (Luke 4:23)
Portion (Psalm 119:57)
Strength (Psalm 18:1; 28:7; 46:1; 73:26)

Stand up and praise the LORD your God, who is from everlasting to everlasting. Blessed be your glorious name, and may it be exalted above all blessing and praise. Nehemiah 9:5

~~~~~~

### Monday – Find a word
Choose a word from the devotion or cited scriptures to reflect on for the week. Some examples: sovereign, righteous, almighty, full, uphold, future, hope, love, obedience. What is your word? _____

Search your Bible commentary. What verses use your word? List them here. Use your journal if you need additional space.

_____
_____
_____
_____

### Tuesday – Define
Choose one to two words to define and then reread the scriptures, replacing the word with the definition. How did it take your understanding to a new level?

### Wednesday – Translate
Choose two or three different Bible translations. Read the Monday verses (cited in the devotional or found in your study) in each translation. Now write them in your journal.

### Thursday – Go the Distance
Read the entire chapter of your favorite verse for the week.

### Friday – Prayer
Close your eyes and talk to God or write out your prayer in your journal.

# Week 13 ~ Warning! Flammable!

**Consult God's instruction and the testimony of warning. If anyone does not speak according to this word, they have no light of dawn. Isaiah 8:20**

I went to check on our daughter, who had been in the shower for an extended period of time, and immediately noticed she was reaching for the shaving cream. "You do not need that," I told her. She replied, "No, you don't understand, I'm trying to cool it off. I've been in the shower for a long time and it says not to put it in extreme heat or it could explode." I could see on her face the sincere worry that her long, hot shower might make that flammable shaving cream explode!

**Many of them will stumble; they will fall and be broken, they will be snared and captured. Bind up this testimony of warning and seal up God's instruction among my disciples. Isaiah 8:15-16**

What if we read God's word and take His warnings and laws that seriously? What if we take His word to heart and approach it with care and careful consideration? What if we trust that He knows best and there is a reason He is Creator of the universe and not us? How different would our lives, our communities and our world look if we listened and obeyed God's word with a hint of fear? He gives instructions and guidance for living in a Christ-like way. For every challenge, He has a solution. For every battle, a weapon. For every trial, an advocate. Our world is quick to disregard the warnings and place the blame, but slow to seek wise counsel and rectify the problems.

Evangelical pastor and Christian author, John Ortberg said, "Most Christians are trying, rather than training to live the Christian life." If you try to run a 5K race without training, you will surely fail. But with proper training, you'll have the endurance to complete the challenge on race day. If we are trying only to do the right thing, we will fail. We cannot give up. We must start training to live a life that looks more like Christ's by digging deeper into His word, finding Him in the ordinary and seeking Him first in all we do.

**Fix these words of mine in your hearts and minds; tie them as symbols on your hands and bind them on your foreheads. Deuteronomy 11:18**

~~~~~~

### Monday – Find a word

Choose a word from the devotion or cited scriptures to reflect on for the week. Some examples: sovereign, righteous, almighty, full, uphold, future, hope, love, obedience. What is your word? _____

Search your Bible commentary. What verses use your word? List them here. Use your journal if you need additional space.

_____
_____
_____
_____

### Tuesday – Define

Choose one to two words to define and then reread the scriptures, replacing the word with the definition. How did it take your understanding to a new level?

### Wednesday – Translate

Choose two or three different Bible translations. Read the Monday verses (cited in the devotional or found in your study) in each translation. Now write them in your journal.

### Thursday – Go the Distance

Read the entire chapter of your favorite verse for the week.

### Friday – Prayer

Close your eyes and talk to God or write out your prayer in your journal.

# Week 14 ~ Symbiotic

I'm singing my heart out to God – what a victory! He pitched horse and rider into the sea. God is my strength, God is my song, and, yes! God is my salvation. This is the kind of God I have and I'm telling the world! This is the God of my father – I'm spreading the news far and wide! God is a fighter, pure God, through and through. (excerpt from Exodus 15:1 – The Message)

"Mommy, we have a symbiotic relationship," my son declared as we were driving. "What do you mean?" I asked, trying to recall those science lessons from so long ago. "Well, you needed me to sweep the porch and, when I did, you gave me money. We have a symbiotic relationship. Just like the clownfish and sea anemone." I was glad my husband and daughter were in the car to hear this one or else no one would have believed me.

For those of us who cannot remember all those old science lessons, "a symbiotic relationship is when one organism lives off another organism without causing harm to either organism. In most cases, one organism benefits from the relationship and the other is not affected at all." (Askkids.com)

Once we, too, were foolish and disobedient. We were misled and became slaves to many lusts and pleasures. Our lives were full of evil and envy, and we hated each other. Titus 3:3 (NLT)

I began thinking back on my life the way it was before I came into daily communication and fellowship with the Lord. It wasn't pretty and there were no benefits to my pridefulness as I tried to navigate this world on my own, without direction. I am so thankful God has given us His living word so that we can "live" forgiven, encouraged, empowered and meaningful lives in His name!

Sometimes I still feel like a parasite, draining the host dry with constant prayers, requests, conversations and needs. I praise Him that He is all powerful, mighty, unchangeable and bigger than any of my problems or needs. He never sleeps or slumbers, never tires of hearing our praises or petitions and NEVER stops loving us.

Yes, life gets tough (sometimes, even unbearable), but God promises protection (Psalm 91). Not removal, but protection. Jesus paid the ultimate price on the cross for us. I am so thankful that He lives inside me and fills my heart with joy, peace and love so that I can share it with others. Without the love of Christ dwelling in me, it would be impossible to love others as He has called me to. Christ has claimed victory over death. At the minimum, we should try to live our lives to honor Him, His word and His sacrifice. Will you join me?

**… not looking to your own interests but each of you to the interests of the others. In your relationships with one another, have the same mindset as Christ Jesus: Philippians 2:4-5**

~~~~~~

### Monday – Find a word

Choose a word from the devotion or cited scriptures to reflect on for the week. Some examples: sovereign, righteous, almighty, full, uphold, future, hope, love, obedience. What is your word? _____

Search your Bible commentary. What verses use your word? List them here. Use your journal if you need additional space.

_____
_____
_____

### Tuesday – Define
Choose one to two words to define and then reread the scriptures, replacing the word with the definition. How did it take your understanding to a new level?

### Wednesday – Translate
Choose two or three different Bible translations. Read the Monday verses (cited in the devotional or found in your study) in each translation. Now write them in your journal.

### Thursday – Go the Distance
Read the entire chapter of your favorite verse for the week.

### Friday – Prayer
Close your eyes and talk to God or write out your prayer in your journal.

# Week 15 ~ God Hates?

"Oh, I hate it when that happens," I said under my breath. "Mommy," my son quickly reminded me, "we don't say 'hate' in this house!" Kids never let you off the hook. (If you are a mom, you know what I mean.) But he was right. We don't use that word in our house because it isn't kind and it isn't a word I want my children to grow accustomed to. It's hard enough to teach your children that God has called us to love our enemy and turn the other cheek.

**Do not bear a grudge against others, but settle your differences with them, so that you will not commit a sin because of them. Do not take revenge on others or continue to hate them, but love your neighbors as you love yourself. I am the Lord. Leviticus 19:17-19**

God has called us to love as He does and leave any revenge in His hands. For this reason, these verses from Proverbs really struck me.

**There are six things the LORD hates, seven that are detestable to him: haughty eyes, a lying tongue, hands that shed innocent blood, a heart that devises wicked schemes, feet that are quick to rush into evil, a false witness who pours out lies and a person who stirs up conflict in the community. Proverbs 6:16-19**

I looked up six or seven Bible translations of this passage to see if the word "hate" appeared in them. It did! It occurred to me that we tend to focus on God's love for us, His promises and His truths. These are all important, but so too are the things our God hates. The verses are a good reminder that we need to maintain a healthy respect for our Lord and Savior. We are to be God-fearing and remember His power and glory above all things. This world accepts – even celebrates – the sinful characteristics listed in Proverbs, such as arrogance, deceit, lying, evil, wickedness and troublemaking, but our God and His rules are to be taken seriously.

**Look for it as hard as you would for silver or some hidden treasure. If you do, you will know what it means to fear the Lord and you will succeed in learning about God. It is the Lord who gives wisdom; from him come knowledge and understanding. Proverbs 2:5-6**

For further study, I've included Proverbs 6:16-19 from The Message translation. I hope it takes you deeper as you abide in His word.

Here are six things God hates,
and one more that he loathes with a passion:
eyes that are arrogant,
a tongue that lies,
hands that murder the innocent,
a heart that hatches evil plots,
feet that race down a wicked track,
a mouth that lies under oath,
a troublemaker in the family. Proverbs 6:16-19 (The Message)

~~~~~~

### Monday – Find a word
Choose a word from the devotion or cited scriptures to reflect on for the week. Some examples: sovereign, righteous, almighty, full, uphold, future, hope, love, obedience. What is your word? _____

Search your Bible commentary. What verses use your word? List them here. Use your journal if you need additional space.

_____
_____
_____
_____

### Tuesday – Define
Choose one to two words to define and then reread the scriptures, replacing the word with the definition. How did it take your understanding to a new level?

### Wednesday – Translate
Choose two or three different Bible translations. Read the Monday verses (cited in the devotional or found in your study) in each translation. Now write them in your journal.

### Thursday – Go the Distance
Read the entire chapter of your favorite verse for the week.

### Friday – Prayer
Close your eyes and talk to God or write out your prayer in your journal.

# Week 16 ~ Abide

**If you remain in me and my words remain in you, ask whatever you wish, and it will be done for you. John 15:7**

My son and I were discussing some bad news, and who'd break it to my daughter, when he said, "Mommy, you should tell her because you always find a way to lower her *out-of-controlness*!" I was amazed he thought that, because I don't see it that way at all. In fact, sometimes I think I raise her "*out-of-controlness.*"

**Surely your goodness and love will follow me all the days of my life, and I will dwell in the house of the LORD forever. Psalm 23:6**

When life seems to spiral out of control or my challenges seem impossible to overcome, I think that God thinks way too highly of me. I then remember that He formed me in my mother's womb and knows my heart even better than I know it myself. My earthly flesh tends to spiral into the "*out-of-controlness*" zone, but I am reminded through God's word to abide, to dwell and to remain in Him and He will provide, protect and proclaim for me.

**Let the message of Christ dwell among you richly as you teach and admonish one another with all wisdom through psalms, hymns, and songs from the Spirit, singing to God with gratitude in your hearts. Colossians 3:16**

I learned that "the word" translates literally in Greek to "face-to-face with God." What a marvelous thing to remember as we try to overcome our earthly reactions by staying grounded in the word of our Father.

In His word, God talks a lot about abiding, which means to dwell or reside in a place or to await something or someone. I cannot think of anyone I'd rather reside with or wait for than our Lord and Savior. The One who created the written word so we could have a face-to-face relationship with Him. The One who allowed His son to die for us so the Holy Spirit could dwell in us.

**For in the day of trouble he will keep me safe in his dwelling; he will hide me in the shelter of his sacred tent and set me high upon a rock. Psalm 27:5**

Rejoice today! We have a Provider, a Protector and One who will proclaim His word through us to all the nations if we remain in Him and allow Him to dwell in us.

**I am the vine; you are the branches. If you remain in me and I in you, you will bear much fruit; apart from me you can do nothing. If you do not remain in me, you are like a branch that is thrown away and withers; such branches are picked up, thrown into the fire and burned. John 15:5-6**

~~~~~~

### Monday – Find a word
Choose a word from the devotion or cited scriptures to reflect on for the week. Some examples: sovereign, righteous, almighty, full, uphold, future, hope, love, obedience. What is your word? _____

Search your Bible commentary. What verses use your word? List them here. Use your journal if you need additional space.

_____
_____
_____

### Tuesday – Define
Choose one to two words to define and then reread the scriptures, replacing the word with the definition. How did it take your understanding to a new level?

### Wednesday – Translate
Choose two or three different Bible translations. Read the Monday verses (cited in the devotional or found in your study) in each translation. Now write them in your journal.

### Thursday – Go the Distance
Read the entire chapter of your favorite verse for the week.

### Friday – Prayer
Close your eyes and talk to God or write out your prayer in your journal.

# Week 17 ~ Just Breathe

Then one who looked like a man touched my lips, and I opened my mouth and began to speak. I said to the one standing before me, "I am overcome with anguish because of the vision, my lord, and I feel very weak. How can I, your servant, talk with you, my lord? My strength is gone and I can hardly breathe." Again the one who looked like a man touched me and gave me strength. Daniel 10:16-18

Sometimes, when our children are hurt, they get so upset they forget to breathe. My husband and I have to say, "Breathe! Take a breath! Breathe!" so they won't pass out. Have you ever experienced a time in your life when something seemed too overwhelming to face or so scary that you had to remind yourself to *just breathe*, to *take a deep breath*? Unfortunately, I can answer *yes* to this question. How do we remember to take our worries and fears to God first? To take a breath and find the peace and trust we need in His word?

**Again Jesus said, "Peace be with you! As the Father has sent me, I am sending you." And with that he breathed on them and said, "Receive the Holy Spirit. If you forgive anyone's sins, their sins are forgiven; if you do not forgive them, they are not forgiven." John 20:21-23**

When we are faced with challenges, we should fill up our hearts and minds with God's word and promises. If we do this we will hear His still, small voice reminding us of His presence and words of comfort and peace. Receive His peace and love today. He died so that we would have life. Let's not waste that incredible and sacrificial gift of love from our Father in heaven.

Heavenly Father, giver of all things, creator of all we see and all we don't, Your love for me is astounding and brings me to my knees. I am in awe of You—all You were, all You are and all You will be. Christ Jesus, You dwell in me and I claim Your love and power today. I claim the peace only You can offer. I claim the forgiveness You sacrificed to provide for me. Please use me to draw others to You and give me the strength and courage to seek and serve You daily in a mighty way. In Your holy, holy, holy name I pray. Amen.

Jesus called out with a loud voice, "Father, into your hands I commit my spirit." When he had said this, he breathed his last. Luke 23:46

~~~~~~

### Monday – Find a word
Choose a word from the devotion or cited scriptures to reflect on for the week. Some examples: sovereign, righteous, almighty, full, uphold, future, hope, love, obedience. What is your word? _____

Search your Bible commentary. What verses use your word? List them here. Use your journal if you need additional space.

_____
_____
_____
_____

### Tuesday – Define
Choose one to two words to define and then reread the scriptures, replacing the word with the definition. How did it take your understanding to a new level?

### Wednesday – Translate
Choose two or three different Bible translations. Read the Monday verses (cited in the devotional or found in your study) in each translation. Now write them in your journal.

### Thursday – Go the Distance
Read the entire chapter of your favorite verse for the week.

### Friday – Prayer
Close your eyes and talk to God or write out your prayer in your journal.

# Week 18 ~ Poison

Jesus said to him, "Away from me, Satan! For it is written: 'Worship the Lord your God, and serve him only.' " Matthew 4:10

My son was planning to catch a lizard so he could keep it for a pet. (Yes, I told him if he caught a lizard it could stay for a sleepover, but we'd have to release it the next day.) He informed me that first we had to collect dead bugs so the lizard would have food when it stayed the night. I told him to look in the basement for dead crickets when he said, "Mommy, I thought you sprayed that perfume stuff down there so the crickets wouldn't come in basement." It took me a moment to realize that the "perfume" he was talking about was the scented poison the exterminator sprays every few months to keep bugs out of the house.

And then it hit me! Satan deceives us every day in the same way. He masks the poison of the sins of the flesh. Hurtful words, distrust, worry, fear and other worldly pleasures are covered up with excuses, disclaimers, exceptions and denial to make his poison smell like perfume. The worst part is that we often fall for Satan's lies. In fact, many times we are quicker to believe them than God's truth.

**Some people are like seed along the path, where the word is sown. As soon as they hear it, Satan comes and takes away the word that was sown in them. Mark 4:15**

This is why we must fill our minds, hearts and lives with the word of God. We cannot allow Satan to form a stronghold over us. If we have filled ourselves up with God, there is little room left for poisonous lies.

**But when Jesus turned and looked at his disciples, he rebuked Peter. "Get behind me, Satan!" he said. "You do not have in mind the concerns of God, but merely human concerns." Mark 8:33**

I pray we all focus on the concerns of God this week and not "merely human concerns."

~~~~~~

### Monday – Find a word

Choose a word from the devotion or cited scriptures to reflect on for the week. Some examples: sovereign, righteous, almighty, full, uphold, future, hope, love, obedience. What is your word? _____

Search your Bible commentary. What verses use your word? List them here. Use your journal if you need additional space.

_____
_____
_____
_____

### Tuesday – Define

Choose one to two words to define and then reread the scriptures, replacing the word with the definition. How did it take your understanding to a new level?

### Wednesday – Translate

Choose two or three different Bible translations. Read the Monday verses (cited in the devotional or found in your study) in each translation. Now write them in your journal.

### Thursday – Go the Distance

Read the entire chapter of your favorite verse for the week.

### Friday – Prayer

Close your eyes and talk to God or write out your prayer in your journal.

# Week 19 ~ JOY!

**I have told you this so that my joy may be in you and that your joy may be complete. John 15:11**

You may or may not have had the same experience, but I've found that God speaks to me at times in recurring messages or themes. He weaves a central theme through His word, a sermon, my Bible study, a podcast or conversation. It will pop up everywhere over days and even weeks. He makes it impossible to miss, and I'm so grateful for His love and vigilance. Like a parent reminding his child at each meal to put her napkin in her lap or to share her toy with her sibling, He never gives up on us.

**My lips will shout for joy when I sing praise to you – I, whom you have redeemed. Psalm 71:23**

I once had a week when God sent me many reminders about joy. I'd needed to be reminded of living a joyful life, so I was grateful for His faithfulness. Joy is defined as the "emotion evoked by well-being, success, or good fortune or by the prospect of possessing what one desires." God calls us to be joyful in times of trial and suffering. Unfortunately, I am pretty sure that when I'm in the midst of financial stress, illness, fear or pain, I don't focus first on the feeling of joy, success or good fortune.

**Nehemiah said, "Go and enjoy choice food and sweet drinks, and send some to those who have nothing prepared. This day is sacred to our Lord. Do not grieve, for the joy of the LORD is your strength." Nehemiah 8:10**

When life hits hard, my first response is usually summed up by the antonyms of joy: sadness, sorrow and woe. Thankfully, God's word and truth are hidden in my heart and, through tears or seeds of doubt, they begin to seep out and cover the sadness, sorrow and woe with great joy and gladness. It's through no power or strength of my own that this happens. It's only by the Lord's grace, love and power this is possible. We can be filled with JOY because of Him. We can experience JOY when we worship Him despite our problems. We have JOY when we serve Him. We exude JOY when we find peace and trust in His plan.

Sit with God, talk with Him, hear from Him through His word, listen for His whisper and feel the joy that comes with knowing He is sovereign. Let His truth and word cover your woe, your sadness and your worry with joy.

**I will be filled with joy because of you. I will sing praises to your name, O Most High. Psalm 9:2 (NLT)**

~~~~~~

### Monday – Find a word
Choose a word from the devotion or cited scriptures to reflect on for the week. Some examples: sovereign, righteous, almighty, full, uphold, future, hope, love, obedience. What is your word? _____

Search your Bible commentary. What verses use your word? List them here. Use your journal if you need additional space.

_____
_____
_____
_____

### Tuesday – Define
Choose one to two words to define and then reread the scriptures, replacing the word with the definition. How did it take your understanding to a new level?

### Wednesday – Translate
Choose two or three different Bible translations. Read the Monday verses (cited in the devotional or found in your study) in each translation. Now write them in your journal.

### Thursday – Go the Distance
Read the entire chapter of your favorite verse for the week.

### Friday – Prayer
Close your eyes and talk to God or write out your prayer in your journal.

# Week 20 ~ Sovereign

Ah, Sovereign LORD, you have made the heavens and the earth by your great power and outstretched arm. Nothing is too hard for you. Jeremiah 32:17

I was making cupcakes for the teachers and realized I was out of vegetable oil after I'd started mixing. I told the kids we'd have to ask our neighbor, Mrs. Sarah, for a half cup of vegetable oil. My kids jump at the chance to visit neighbors, so my son started putting on his shoes right away. "I'll do it, I'll do it," he said before his sister could offer. "Slow down," I told him. "Do you know what you're asking for?" He looked up from tying his laces and said, "Yes! A half a cup of fish to boil!"

How great you are, Sovereign LORD! There is no one like you, and there is no God but you, as we have heard with our own ears. 2 Samuel 7:22

We get in a hurry sometimes. We rush into a task or something that seems like a good project without first getting a clear picture of what the Lord wants from us. We forget that God is sovereign. His plan should come before ours. We don't stop, we don't ask, we don't pray for discernment and we don't listen for His whisper. We rush, we decide without His input, we try to rule our own territory.

He was driven away from people and given the mind of an animal; he lived with the wild donkeys and ate grass like the ox; and his body was drenched with the dew of heaven, until he acknowledged that the Most High God is sovereign over all kingdoms on earth and sets over them anyone he wishes. Daniel 5:21

Hundreds of times in the Bible we run across the phrase "sovereign Lord" (especially in Ezekiel). Have you thought about what that really means?

Sovereignty is defined as "the quality of having supreme, independent authority over a geographic area, such as a territory." I have read this word thousands of times when studying scripture, but it's tough to give it a biblical definition. In fact, "sovereign" is more than a word when it relates to our Lord and Savior – it's a concept. We hear "God is sovereign," but what does that mean? Sovereignty is also defined as supreme power, dominance and absolute superlative quality, and its synonyms include all-sufficient, irresistible, overwhelming, jurisdiction and mastery.

My favorite is irresistible. Isn't God irresistible? I have found that His sovereignty, His mastery, His all-sufficiency and His dominance are irresistible. Did I ever think I would say that? Honestly, no! For so many years I wanted to remain in charge of my life. I wanted to be in absolute control of my actions and decisions, but He waited patiently on the sidelines while I fumbled, tumbled and messed up. That's what happens when we try to rule our territory instead of letting our sovereign God do it. Are you ready to accept his sovereignty?

**When they heard this, they raised their voices together in prayer to God. "Sovereign Lord," they said, "you made the heavens and the earth and the sea, and everything in them. Acts 4:24**

~~~~~~

### Monday – Find a word
Choose a word from the devotion or cited scriptures to reflect on for the week. Some examples: sovereign, righteous, almighty, full, uphold, future, hope, love, obedience. What is your word? _____
Search your Bible commentary. What verses use your word? List them here. Use your journal if you need additional space.
_____
_____
_____

### Tuesday – Define
Choose one to two words to define and then reread the scriptures, replacing the word with the definition. How did it take your understanding to a new level?

### Wednesday – Translate
Choose two or three different Bible translations. Read the Monday verses (cited in the devotional or found in your study) in each translation. Now write them in your journal.

### Thursday – Go the Distance
Read the entire chapter of your favorite verse for the week.

### Friday – Prayer
Close your eyes and talk to God or write out your prayer in your journal.

# Week 21 ~ Above the Noise

But now, this is what the LORD says – he who created you, Jacob, he who formed you, Israel: "Do not fear, for I have redeemed you; I have summoned you by name; you are mine." Isaiah 43:1

Since I am not a coffee drinker, I make a fruit smoothie every morning for breakfast. As you can imagine, our blenders get a lot of use. In fact, we had to purchase a new blender because the old one gave out from all the work. The replacement blender is amazing. It sounds like a race car when you start it, but it gets the job done. Some mornings, I love to turn on that loud blender because it drowns out all the noise around me for 45 seconds. My husband on his phone, the kids arguing about who gets to brush teeth first, the phone ringing and the never-ending questions about breakfast or the location of shoes. Yes, sometimes those 45 seconds of high-octave noise is truly welcome.

When you pass through the waters, I will be with you; and when you pass through the rivers, they will not sweep over you. When you walk through the fire, you will not be burned; the flames will not set you ablaze. For I am the LORD your God, the Holy One of Israel, your Savior; Isaiah 43:2-3

Although this works for brief moments in the morning, the use of noise to cover more noise is not the greatest option. It's the path we often choose in life, however. We try to drown our worries, pain, betrayal, fear and sadness with the temporary distractions of shopping, busyness, denial, etc. It takes a lot of effort to rise above the noise in this world. I don't know about you, but I'm interested in a permanent fix, not one that lasts for 45 seconds.

Our permanent fix is God. We are not capable of handling life's obstacles without His strength, His courage, His love and His power. I read once (author unknown) that "His voice is for the ear of love, and love is intent upon hearing even the faintest whispers." He offers a place above the noise where we can rest in His word and His promises. Meet Him in the pages of His spoken, living word. He is waiting for you to join Him there.

You, God, are my God, earnestly I seek you; I thirst for you, my whole being longs for you, in a dry and parched land where there is no water. Psalm 63:1

~~~~~~

### Monday – Find a word

Choose a word from the devotion or cited scriptures to reflect on for the week. Some examples: sovereign, righteous, almighty, full, uphold, future, hope, love, obedience. What is your word? _____

Search your Bible commentary. What verses use your word? List them here. Use your journal if you need additional space.

_____
_____
_____
_____

### Tuesday – Define

Choose one to two words to define and then reread the scriptures, replacing the word with the definition. How did it take your understanding to a new level?

### Wednesday – Translate

Choose two or three different Bible translations. Read the Monday verses (cited in the devotional or found in your study) in each translation. Now write them in your journal.

### Thursday – Go the Distance

Read the entire chapter of your favorite verse for the week.

### Friday – Prayer

Close your eyes and talk to God or write out your prayer in your journal.

# Week 22 ~ Take Cover

These (trials) have come so that your faith – of greater worth than gold, which perishes even though refined by fire – may be proved genuine and may result in praise, glory and honor when Jesus Christ is revealed. 1 Peter 1:7

Change happens fast, and you never know what's around the corner. Pastor Charles Swindoll, said in his sermon on the book of Job, "We never know ahead of time God's plan for us, so be ready for anything." Have you ever read a more true statement?

My husband and I made some life-changing decisions, about career and lifestyle, based on assurances that we believed and trusted. We were later blindsided when those assurances were yanked out from under us. I held back tears as I discussed this turn of events with my daughter, and I told her I felt like crawling into bed and hiding under the covers for a little while.

We all have those days, don't we? Those days we wake up wishing we could hide from the facts, from reality and truth. But that's not an option because the problem will not go away just because we hide or pretend it's not there. My son had been saying "I surrender" for days because of a game he played with friends at school. He asked me what it meant to surrender, and I told him it meant to give up or give in to the power of another. So, I asked him why he thought people surrendered. He said, "Because they are scared!"

Many times, we are not able to surrender to God until fear sets in. When I looked up surrender, found it meant not only to "declare yourself defeated" but also to "give up possession of something" and "give something out of courtesy." What would it look like if we gave God our lives and possessions out of courtesy?

**Whoever finds their life will lose it, and whoever loses their life for my sake will find it. Matthew 10:39**

When we give up possession of our lives and our plans, we discover a life in Christ. We find that what He has to offer is so much more than we could ever imagine. His peace, strength, grace, truth, comfort, forgiveness and love endure forever.

The troubles, the pain and the problems we have here will not endure forever, but our God and His promises remain true from everlasting to everlasting.

**Give thanks to the LORD, for he is good; his love endures forever. 1 Chronicles 16:34**

Be ready for anything!

~~~~~~

### Monday – Find a word
Choose a word from the devotion or cited scriptures to reflect on for the week. Some examples: sovereign, righteous, almighty, full, uphold, future, hope, love, obedience. What is your word? _____

Search your Bible commentary. What verses use your word? List them here. Use your journal if you need additional space.

_____
_____
_____
_____


### Tuesday – Define
Choose one to two words to define and then reread the scriptures, replacing the word with the definition. How did it take your understanding to a new level?

### Wednesday – Translate
Choose two or three different Bible translations. Read the Monday verses (cited in the devotional or found in your study) in each translation. Now write them in your journal.

### Thursday – Go the Distance
Read the entire chapter of your favorite verse for the week.

### Friday – Prayer
Close your eyes and talk to God or write out your prayer in your journal.

# Week 23 ~ Do-Over

Then he called the crowd to him along with his disciples and said: "Whoever wants to be my disciple must deny themselves and take up their cross and follow me. For whoever wants to save their life will lose it, but whoever loses their life for me and for the gospel will save it. What good is it for someone to gain the whole world, yet forfeit their soul?" Mark 8:34-36

Have you ever had one of those days? One of those days you had all planned out, but then nothing went the way you wanted it to? When I'm sideswiped by chaos or unexpected problems – and I know I have no control over them – my mind still can become dizzy with worry.

"Hand it over to the Lord," my heart screams as my mind tugs back for control. Denying the god of "me, myself and I" can be a struggle some days. There are times I wish I could hit the pause or rewind button and start over. "I need a do-over," my husband and I say. Often, a "do-over" seems like a more appealing option than sticking it out where my circumstances have landed me.

**My steps have held to your paths; my feet have not stumbled. Psalm 17:5**

But I wonder what opportunities I'd miss if I could pause, rewind or start over. Would I grow in Christ if I always took the easy way out? Would I see Him at work in my daily life if I never stumbled off His path? More importantly, would my life shine in such a way that led others to Christ? I feel confident in answering "no" to all of these questions.

**For your ways are in full view of the LORD, and he examines all your paths. Proverbs 5:21**

The Lord knows what obstacles are ahead of us because He is walking with us. He is able to keep us from stumbling if we allow Him to help. He will reveal Himself to us through words of encouragement and peace if we seek Him through His word. The good news is that we do not need a "do-over" because Christ took care of that when he died for me and for you on the cross.

**having canceled the charge of our legal indebtedness, which stood against us and condemned us; he has taken it away, nailing it to the cross. Colossians 2:14**

~~~~~~

### Monday – Find a word
Choose a word from the devotion or cited scriptures to reflect on for the week. Some examples: sovereign, righteous, almighty, full, uphold, future, hope, love, obedience. What is your word? _____

Search your Bible commentary. What verses use your word? List them here. Use your journal if you need additional space.

_____
_____
_____
_____

### Tuesday – Define
Choose one to two words to define and then reread the scriptures, replacing the word with the definition. How did it take your understanding to a new level?

### Wednesday – Translate
Choose two or three different Bible translations. Read the Monday verses (cited in the devotional or found in your study) in each translation. Now write them in your journal.

### Thursday – Go the Distance
Read the entire chapter of your favorite verse for the week.

### Friday – Prayer
Close your eyes and talk to God or write out your prayer in your journal.

# Week 24 ~ Detour

Look after each other so that none of you fails to receive the grace of God. Watch out that no poisonous root of bitterness grows up to trouble you, corrupting many. Hebrews 12:15

It had been a great day. Everything on my to-do list had been accomplished, things were in order and the sun was out after a week of cloudy, cold weather. I sat content and waited patiently for my son in the preschool carpool line. I was ready to kiss him and give him my full attention as he told me about his day. Then he got in the car and it was like I had hit a bump in the smooth road I'd been on all day. Detour!

My son started in immediately about how someone in his class had laughed at him, how terrible it was, how that child should have gotten in trouble, how it hurt his feelings. It went on and on. I tried to explain to him that sometimes people laugh with us – not at us – and in the situation he was describing, I knew this was the case. But there was no convincing him. He dwelled on it all the way home, all afternoon, told his sister about it as soon as we picked her up, and he was still in a knot about it when my husband got home from work. He just could not let it go. No matter how I explained it, how much we discussed it and rationalized it, he WOULD NOT forgive or let go.

My son had allowed that situation to ruin his day, my day, his sister's day and our entire evening. I thought of all the times I'd been in a similar situation. Times when I had allowed a circumstance, a harsh word, a misunderstanding or a situation to ruin my day and the day of those around me. Why do we do this? Why can we not see beyond our agitation and realize that we give the situation or person a power over us that we should not allow? These instances plant a seed of bitterness in us, and then we water the seed, give it sunshine, fertilizer and allow it to grow. We should recognize instead that the plant is really a weed that needs to be plucked so it doesn't infiltrate our hearts and minds.

**Get rid of all bitterness, rage and anger, brawling and slander, along with every form of malice. Ephesians 4:31**

The truth is that we allow a person or event to have power over us because we don't take our problems to God. We cannot do it without Him, but with Him WE CAN move forward. He can give us the grace, strength, courage and power we need to forgive and dismiss. We must pluck the weed of bitterness that is sprouting before it takes root in our day, our relationships and our lives. But, we have to ASK Him for help. He is there on the sidelines waiting for an invitation. Will you ask for His help? Will you knock so the door will be opened to you? Will you seek so that you may find?

**Ask and it will be given to you; seek and you will find; knock and the door will be opened to you. For everyone who asks receives; the one who seeks finds; and to the one who knocks, the door will be opened. Matthew 7:7-8**

~~~~~~

### Monday – Find a word
Choose a word from the devotion or cited scriptures to reflect on for the week. Some examples: sovereign, righteous, almighty, full, uphold, future, hope, love, obedience. What is your word? _____

Search your Bible commentary. What verses use your word? List them here. Use your journal if you need additional space.
_____
_____
_____

### Tuesday – Define
Choose one to two words to define and then reread the scriptures, replacing the word with the definition. How did it take your understanding to a new level?

### Wednesday – Translate
Choose two or three different Bible translations. Read the Monday verses (cited in the devotional or found in your study) in each translation. Now write them in your journal.

### Thursday – Go the Distance
Read the entire chapter of your favorite verse for the week.

### Friday – Prayer
Close your eyes and talk to God or write out your prayer in your journal.

# Week 25 ~ Trash

**Create in me a pure heart, O God, and renew a steadfast spirit within me. Psalm 51:10**

A "not-so-fresh" smell had taken over my car. There was no more ignoring it or covering it with air freshener. So, while getting gas, I decided it was time to clean out the trashcan I keep in the backseat for the kids. Whew! If you've ever been a mom or had kids in your car for any length of time, you can imagine all the things that came out of that trashcan. Some recognizable and some NOT!

**Godly sorrow brings repentance that leads to salvation and leaves no regret, but worldly sorrow brings death. 2 Corinthians 7:10**

Repentance is vital in our walk with God. Daily repentance. If our hearts go uncleased, we can start acting "not so fresh" ourselves. Attitudes, anger, restlessness, regret or whatever else you have rotting in your heart can permeate your life and the lives of those around you. Ignoring it will not work. Covering it up will not work. Well, it might for a little while, but eventually you won't be able to stand yourself or, worse, others will not want to be around you.

**The Lord is not slow in keeping his promise, as some understand slowness. Instead he is patient with you, not wanting anyone to perish, but everyone to come to repentance. 2 Peter 3:9**

The good news is that, just like the trashcan in my car, we can empty out the trash we hold in our hearts EVERY DAY! God is waiting for us to drop it at His feet, accept His love, His forgiveness and His grace. His great love for us is a mystery to me. I am not capable of understanding it, but it is real and available to us if we just ask.

### GodChick's L-O-V-E!

L = let it go, O = on our knees, V = very passionately, E = every day!

~~~~~~

### Monday – Find a word

Choose a word from the devotion or cited scriptures to reflect on for the week. Some examples: sovereign, righteous, almighty, full, uphold, future, hope, love, obedience. What is your word? _____

Search your Bible commentary. What verses use your word? List them here. Use your journal if you need additional space.

_____
_____
_____
_____

### Tuesday – Define

Choose one to two words to define and then reread the scriptures, replacing the word with the definition. How did it take your understanding to a new level?

### Wednesday – Translate

Choose two or three different Bible translations. Read the Monday verses (cited in the devotional or found in your study) in each translation. Now write them in your journal.

### Thursday – Go the Distance

Read the entire chapter of your favorite verse for the week.

### Friday – Prayer

Close your eyes and talk to God or write out your prayer in your journal.

# Week 26 ~ It's an Honor

**My salvation and my honor depend on God; he is my mighty rock, my refuge. Psalm 62:7**

"It is an honor to meet you." "It is my honor to host this event for you." "It is an honor to be in your presence." "I am doing this in honor of . . . ."

Most of us have heard or said one of the above statements. As a verb, the word honor means to hold in honor or high respect; to revere. Who is it that you honor? For whom do you have a high respect? Whom do you revere? Is there someone on the list above God?

Sometimes I struggle with the direction or situation that God has chosen for me. Whether it's financial, personal, professional or spiritual. *I question. I argue. I dismiss. I disregard. I ignore. It is frustrating. It is not the plan I had in mind. It is not easy. It is too scary.* Does any of this sound familiar or I am alone in the struggle?

**Therefore, since we have these promises, dear friends, let us purify ourselves from everything that contaminates body and spirit, perfecting holiness out of reverence for God. 2 Corinthians 7:1**

When I stop to consider all the good, the wisdom, the love and the growth our God wants us to experience, my feelings turn to shame and repentance. Our God knows what is best. His ways are good and His sight is above ours. When they're not ours, we sometimes find it difficult to honor God's choices and direction for us. When we submit to His will and are thankful for His blessings, He rewards us.

Our honor and reverence should be for HIM! It is an honor to serve You, Father. It is an honor to welcome You into my heart, Lord. It is an honor to have the opportunity to sit at Your feet and experience Your forgiveness and grace. It is an honor to accept this great love You have for me. It is an honor to know that You know me by name. It is an honor to experience this pain so I can grow in You and draw closer to You.

Father, it is an honor to know You and to have the opportunity to share You with others. Thank You for this honor.

Is it your honor?

But with you there is forgiveness, so that we can, with reverence, serve you.
Psalm 130:4

~~~~~~

### Monday – Find a word
Choose a word from the devotion or cited scriptures to reflect on for the week. Some examples: sovereign, righteous, almighty, full, uphold, future, hope, love, obedience. What is your word? _____

Search your Bible commentary. What verses use your word? List them here. Use your journal if you need additional space.

_____
_____
_____
_____

### Tuesday – Define
Choose one to two words to define and then reread the scriptures, replacing the word with the definition. How did it take your understanding to a new level?

### Wednesday – Translate
Choose two or three different Bible translations. Read the Monday verses (cited in the devotional or found in your study) in each translation. Now write them in your journal.

### Thursday – Go the Distance
Read the entire chapter of your favorite verse for the week.

### Friday – Prayer
Close your eyes and talk to God or write out your prayer in your journal.

## Week 27 ~ Hub

My phone rang and it was my Dad. Mom was out of town and he needed to know where he was supposed to go to order his tuxedo. My husband beeped in on my phone call to check our schedule for Saturday so he could make plans. A little while later, I received an e-mail from a friend asking my opinion about a Bible study she was interested in. My son walks in, "Mommy, where is my remote-control car?" Well, you get the idea. If you are a mom, wife, daughter, sister or friend, you probably know how it feels to be the "go-to" girl. Our minds have to run like a central command center.

Hub is defined as "a center around which other things revolve or from which they radiate; a focus of activity, authority." God's place in our lives should always be the hub – the center! He should be in the middle of all we do, all we think and all we plan. When activities and to-do lists become the hub of my life, God is pushed aside. He often gets pushed to the back or side. It takes effort, time, devotion, trust and grace on my part to put Him back into His rightful place in my life.

How do we know God wants to be in the middle or center of our lives? God shows us in the book of Genesis. Where were the tree of life and the tree of knowledge of good and evil?

**And the LORD God made all kinds of trees grow out of the ground – trees that were pleasing to the eye and good for food. In the <u>middle</u> of the garden were the tree of life and the tree of the knowledge of good and evil. Genesis 2:9**
Where did God instruct Joshua to have the Israelites collect 12 stones for the memorial to the people of Israel?

**So the Israelites did as Joshua commanded them. They took twelve stones from the <u>middle</u> of the Jordan, according to the number of the tribes of the Israelites, as the LORD had told Joshua; and they carried them over with them to their camp, where they put them down. Joshua 4:8**

In Revelations, where is the lamb located on the throne?

For the Lamb at the <u>center</u> of the throne will be their shepherd; he will lead them to springs of living water. And God will wipe away every tear from their eyes. Revelation 7:17

Notice these things did not happen on the sidelines or in the back! References throughout the Bible to God being in the center and middle astound me. I encourage you to continue digging into the scriptures to find more.

~~~~~~

### Monday – Find a word
Choose a word from the devotion or cited scriptures to reflect on for the week. Some examples: sovereign, righteous, almighty, full, uphold, future, hope, love, obedience. What is your word? _____

Search your Bible commentary. What verses use your word? List them here. Use your journal if you need additional space.
_____
_____
_____
_____

### Tuesday – Define
Choose one to two words to define and then reread the scriptures, replacing the word with the definition. How did it take your understanding to a new level?

### Wednesday – Translate
Choose two or three different Bible translations. Read the Monday verses (cited in the devotional or found in your study) in each translation. Now write them in your journal.

### Thursday – Go the Distance
Read the entire chapter of your favorite verse for the week.

### Friday – Prayer
Close your eyes and talk to God or write out your prayer in your journal.

# Week 28 ~ Even Mommies Have Boogers!

"Oh, I just hate that," I mumbled under my breath as my son happened to walk by. Typically we do not use the word "hate" in our house. Like any good kid, he took the opportunity and ran with it. He gave me a short lecture with a reminder that we do not use words like "hate" in our house and then an explanation as to why I needed to say I was sorry. (Yes, he keeps me in line.)

This, I thought, is a great opportunity to have the "mommy and daddy are not perfect" talk with my son and daughter. The conversation led me to tell them that even mommies have boogers and make mistakes. Our children often think we're perfect and don't make mistakes. They look up to us and think we are superheroes. That can make us feel great inside – even if we know it's not true. But we do our kids and other women a disservice if we allow them to believe this illusion of perfection. They need to hear that we make mistakes and have learned lessons from those mistakes. They need to hear us ask for forgiveness and to offer forgiveness when someone has hurt us.

Have you heard another mother yell at her kids or a wife confess she had a meltdown and cried because she couldn't keep up with everything? Did you feel a sense of relief because you realized you weren't the only one on the planet who had (or was) experiencing that same thing? Who was not perfect?

The Bible is full of amazing people and stories of how they served the Lord. However, other than Jesus, not one of them was perfect. They all made mistakes. In **Jonah 1:1-3**, God asks Jonah to go and speak to His people about their sins, and he runs away from God. In **Job 2:7-10**, Job's wife tells him to "curse God and die!" because Job is in so much pain from the sores on his body and she cannot stand to see him suffer any longer. In **2 Samuel 11:1-4**, David is overwhelmed by the desires of the flesh and commits adultery. In **Ruth 1:20-21**, Naomi blames the Lord for all her loss and changes her name to Mara (which means bitter). I could go on, but I'm sure you get the point. Take some time during your week to look up these verses and read more about each of them. They are all amazing stories.

These people are the rock stars of the Bible and they ran from God, told loved ones to curse Him, broke His commandments and blamed Him for their loss – but they also loved Him! They recognized their weaknesses, asked forgiveness and found strength in the Lord again. We all mess up, we have moments of weakness, we lose our way, our faith falters and we lean on others instead of Him. Yes, we all have boogers, but God loves us anyway! Praise the Lord!

**Therefore, my friends, I want you to know that through Jesus the forgiveness of sins is proclaimed to you. Acts 13:38**

~~~~~~

### Monday – Find a word
Choose a word from the devotion or cited scriptures to reflect on for the week. Some examples: sovereign, righteous, almighty, full, uphold, future, hope, love, obedience. What is your word? _____

Search your Bible commentary. What verses use your word? List them here. Use your journal if you need additional space.

_____
_____
_____
_____

### Tuesday – Define
Choose one to two words to define and then reread the scriptures, replacing the word with the definition. How did it take your understanding to a new level?

### Wednesday – Translate
Choose two or three different Bible translations. Read the Monday verses (cited in the devotional or found in your study) in each translation. Now write them in your journal.

### Thursday – Go the Distance
Read the entire chapter of your favorite verse for the week.

### Friday – Prayer
Close your eyes and talk to God or write out your prayer in your journal.

# Week 29 ~Warming up

I was volunteering at church and needed to make some copies for a project. Of course, as soon as it was my turn at the copier, the toner was empty. After replacing the toner, I had to wait for the copier to "warm up." If you've ever used a copier, you know that after every paper jam, toner change and start or stop, it needs to warm up. Making six copies took 20 minutes, but I got it done and the copies looked great with new toner.

**The path of the righteous is like the morning sun, shining ever brighter till the full light of day. But the way of the wicked is like deep darkness; they do not know what makes them stumble. Proverbs 4:18-19**

I like the concept of warming up. It's beneficial to the person who takes the warm-up and to those who wait for a response or action, even if they're frustrated by the time it takes. I wish this concept came naturally to me, but it takes a conscious effort on my part to stop – pause – take it to God and then respond or react.

We live in a fast-paced world that never slows down. If we want to move at a different pace, we have to make it happen ourselves. How would things change if we hit the "warm-up" button and found time for God daily? What if we paused and asked for God's direction and guidance in all we did and said? What if we sat still to hear God's whisper daily? What if we pushed the "warm-up" button before we responded with words or actions?

**Those who consider themselves religious and yet do not keep a tight rein on their tongues deceive themselves, and their religion is worthless. James 1:26**

If we develop the self-discipline to take it all to God first, think of how our marriages and parenting would improve, our friends would benefit and, most importantly, our relationship with the Lord would blossom.

**She speaks with wisdom, and faithful instruction is on her tongue. Proverbs 31:26**

~~~~~~

### Monday – Find a word

Choose a word from the devotion or cited scriptures to reflect on for the week. Some examples: sovereign, righteous, almighty, full, uphold, future, hope, love, obedience. What is your word? _____

Search your Bible commentary. What verses use your word? List them here. Use your journal if you need additional space.

_____
_____
_____
_____

### Tuesday – Define

Choose one to two words to define and then reread the scriptures, replacing the word with the definition. How did it take your understanding to a new level?

### Wednesday – Translate

Choose two or three different Bible translations. Read the Monday verses (cited in the devotional or found in your study) in each translation. Now write them in your journal.

### Thursday – Go the Distance

Read the entire chapter of your favorite verse for the week.

### Friday – Prayer

Close your eyes and talk to God or write out your prayer in your journal.

# Week 30 ~ Shortcut

I was running late to an appointment after helping out a friend, and I do not like to be late! I thought it would be a good idea to take a shortcut I'd seen my husband take a few times. Of course, I got lost and my shortcut turned out to be a "long cut" and cost me more time. The best laid plans, right?

**The world and its desires pass away, but whoever does the will of God lives forever. 1 John 2:7**

While lost, I thought that my "shortcut" was a great example of how we live our lives. We often decide to take our own path instead of God's path. When we choose our path, we should not be surprised by the detour. Looking back, I remember just a few of the unproductive, hurtful and scary outcomes of my own shortcuts. Whether words or actions, they seemed like a great idea at the time but ended up a disaster in one way or another.

I am sure Satan sits there cheering us on when we get the urge to follow our own desires or those of this world over the ones of our Lord and Savior.

**Therefore, since Christ suffered in his body, arm yourselves also with the same attitude, because whoever suffers in the body is done with sin. As a result, they do not live the rest of their earthly lives for evil human desires, but rather for the will of God. 1 Peter 4:1-2**

*"The will of God"*

Read that again. We throw those four words around a lot, but do we think about what they really mean? We are not capable of fathoming what mighty and amazing plans God has in store for us. We don't always see the benefits while traveling the long road. Many times we want to turn around, take the next exit or give up and veer into the ditch. If we focus on God's word, His truth and His great love for us, the long road can be a wonderful journey that draws us closer to Him than we'd ever imagined. His plan really is perfect and He has a plan just for you.

God's voice thunders in marvelous ways; he does great things beyond our understanding. Job 37:5

~~~~~~

### Monday – Find a word

Choose a word from the devotion or cited scriptures to reflect on for the week. Some examples: sovereign, righteous, almighty, full, uphold, future, hope, love, obedience. What is your word? _____

Search your Bible commentary. What verses use your word? List them here. Use your journal if you need additional space.

_____
_____
_____
_____

### Tuesday – Define

Choose one to two words to define and then reread the scriptures, replacing the word with the definition. How did it take your understanding to a new level?

### Wednesday – Translate

Choose two or three different Bible translations. Read the Monday verses (cited in the devotional or found in your study) in each translation. Now write them in your journal.

### Thursday – Go the Distance

Read the entire chapter of your favorite verse for the week.

### Friday – Prayer

Close your eyes and talk to God or write out your prayer in your journal.

# Week 31 ~ Letting Go

Submit to God and be at peace with him; in this way prosperity will come to you. Job 22:21

Many holidays (and often, just life itself) can raise emotions we thought we'd resolved – emotions we believed we'd moved beyond or pushed so far away as to never surface again. Many times, the returning emotion has to do with letting go of something like betrayal, guilt, unmet expectations or a lifestyle you'd grown accustom to living. Are you struggling to let go of anything during this season of life?

These emotions creep up on me when I least expect them and I find myself shocked at what my heart is feeling. Then, the guilt starts in. How can I feel like this and have a heart for God? How can God still love me and use me for His purpose when my selfish heart is in the way? I have learned that being honest with God is the best medicine to restoring my heart from chaos to peace. When I'm able to overcome these human emotions, I know that God is at work because I am not capable of doing it alone.

"Everything is possible for one who believes." Mark 9:23

We have heard many times, "Let go and let God," but how often do we heed that advice? Think of all the benefits we'd receive if we actually did as this saying suggests and let God in and truly let go. Let Him in to heal the pain, take the place of something worldly or simply find rest in His presence and many blessings.

Jesus looked at them and said, "With man this is impossible, but not with God; all things are possible with God." Mark 10:27

It's impossible for us to change our hearts without God's help. I urge you to search your heart for the things you've been holding but need to let go. Go to God with it – the pain, the hurt, the guilt, the embarrassment – take it all. Then,

Pay attention, and listen to me; be silent, and I will speak. Job 33:31

~~~~~~

### Monday – Find a word
Choose a word from the devotion or cited scriptures to reflect on for the week. Some examples: sovereign, righteous, almighty, full, uphold, future, hope, love, obedience. What is your word? _____

Search your Bible commentary. What verses use your word? List them here. Use your journal if you need additional space.

_____
_____
_____
_____

### Tuesday – Define
Choose one to two words to define and then reread the scriptures, replacing the word with the definition. How did it take your understanding to a new level?

### Wednesday – Translate
Choose two or three different Bible translations. Read the Monday verses (cited in the devotional or found in your study) in each translation. Now write them in your journal.

### Thursday – Go the Distance
Read the entire chapter of your favorite verse for the week.

### Friday – Prayer
Close your eyes and talk to God or write out your prayer in your journal.

# Week 32 ~ Pout

**Complain if you must, but don't lash out. Keep your mouth shut, and let your heart do the talking. Build your case before God and wait for his verdict. Psalm 4:4 (The Message)**

Just typing the word "pout" brings to mind an image of my children that makes my eyes roll. I don't know about you, but I have some good pouters in my house! Occasionally, I need to include myself in that category.

**Friends, don't complain about each other. A far greater complaint could be lodged against you, you know. The Judge is standing just around the corner. James 5:9 (The Message)**

Sometimes we see how God has answered the prayers of those around us. We see how He seems to be present in all they do or, when we hear about someone who's remarkably figured out a way to have quiet time EVERY DAY with God, we let our human tendencies take over and pout. When we hear others' stories or testimonies about how God is working or has worked in their lives and blessed them, it can be easy to fall into a trap of jealousy or resentment. We wonder why we cannot experience God this way and why He seems to be leaving us out when it comes to His blessings.

We don't want to hear others talk about how God has blessed them. We want to experience it for ourselves. We desire to bask in His love, His greatness, His miracles, His glory, His unfailing love and His promised blessings for us.
The closer you are to someone, and the more you know about him or her, the more you notice. Think about it. When you bought the car you're driving, did you think everyone else went out and bought the same model? Or did you think you noticed that type of car more because you were driving one? It's the same with God. The more you know Him, His character and His ways, the more you see Him at work in your everyday life. He is involved in every intricate detail of your life and wants you to see Him and seek Him daily.

It can be difficult to resist, but do not pout! If you're not spending the time with God that you feel you should, ask forgiveness, forgive yourself and put a new plan into action. Pray that God will multiply your time and help you put Him into your schedule. If you are angry or resentful because others seem to be more blessed than you, put in on the altar. God can take it! He can take your anger, your pain, your resentment and whatever else you are holding back. Put yourself out there, trust the Lord, get on your knees before Him and take a risk. Get it off your chest and into the light and watch as God begins to work in your life.

You're blessed when you can show people how to cooperate instead of compete or fight. That's when you discover who you really are, and your place in God's family. Matthew 5:9 (The Message)

~~~~~~

### Monday – Find a word
Choose a word from the devotion or cited scriptures to reflect on for the week. Some examples: sovereign, righteous, almighty, full, uphold, future, hope, love, obedience. What is your word? _____
Search your Bible commentary. What verses use your word? List them here. Use your journal if you need additional space.

_____
_____
_____
_____

### Tuesday – Define
Choose one to two words to define and then reread the scriptures, replacing the word with the definition. How did it take your understanding to a new level?

### Wednesday – Translate
Choose two or three different Bible translations. Read the Monday verses (cited in the devotional or found in your study) in each translation. Now write them in your journal.

### Thursday – Go the Distance
Read the entire chapter of your favorite verse for the week.

### Friday – Prayer
Close your eyes and talk to God or write out your prayer in your journal.

# Week 33 ~ Long Story

My son hopped in the car after preschool and announced, "We learned about respect today in chapel." "What did you learn about respect?" I asked. "Well, it's a long story," he replied.

I could not have said it better myself. Teaching, guiding and directing our children to know God is not something we'll ever be able to cross off the list. It *is* a long story that we should never stop telling our children or others. We are called to do so and we cannot let this responsibility fall to the side or leave it for someone else to do.

**Fix these words of mine in your hearts and minds; tie them as symbols on your hands and bind them on your foreheads. Teach them to your children, talking about them when you sit at home and when you walk along the road, when you lie down and when you get up. Write them on the doorframes of your houses and on your gates. Deuteronomy 11:18-20**

We are to live, share, teach and constantly think about the words of the Lord and share them with our children. This takes time, thought, work, study and love. Love for the Lord and love for our children and others. It is easy to let this job/responsibility get lost in the busyness of life.

My godchild called me one weekend to ask some questions about God. She wanted to know if God was magic. She could not understand how He was able to live in her heart, her mom's heart and the hearts of others without there being hundreds of Him. A lot of important things happened for her to discover the answers. First, she asked the questions, which shows her heart for God (and that she is listening in school). Second, her parents helped her find some answers. Third, I responded with scripture and her parents followed through with more discussion.

**Only be careful, and watch yourselves closely so that you do not forget the things your eyes have seen or let them fade from your heart as long as you live. Teach them to your children and to their children after them. Deuteronomy 4:9**

It *is* a long story! Have you missed an opportunity to share the Lord with a child? I encourage you to look for an opportunity every day this week to share a thought or word about God. It may be your own children, grandchildren, the kids standing behind you in the grocery store, neighbors, children in your Sunday school class. God will open the doors and give you the opportunity if you are willing to tell the story and plant the seed.

~~~~~~

### Monday – Find a word

Choose a word from the devotion or cited scriptures to reflect on for the week. Some examples: sovereign, righteous, almighty, full, uphold, future, hope, love, obedience. What is your word? _____

Search your Bible commentary. What verses use your word? List them here. Use your journal if you need additional space.

_____
_____
_____
_____

### Tuesday – Define

Choose one to two words to define and then reread the scriptures, replacing the word with the definition. How did it take your understanding to a new level?

### Wednesday – Translate

Choose two or three different Bible translations. Read the Monday verses (cited in the devotional or found in your study) in each translation. Now write them in your journal.

### Thursday – Go the Distance

Read the entire chapter of your favorite verse for the week.

### Friday – Prayer

Close your eyes and talk to God or write out your prayer in your journal.

## Week 34 ~ Did you see that?

"Did you see me do that?" my son asked his friend as he ran off the basketball court. "Why don't you watch me just in case I do something amazing?" My son didn't want his friend to miss anything great he might do on the court. I wonder how many times God whispers, "Did you see that? I am right here. Did you notice?"

**Joshua told the people, "Consecrate yourselves, for tomorrow the LORD will do amazing things among you." Joshua 3:5**

There are many reasons why we miss out on God's amazing works. Not watching or paying close attention is the easiest answer, but there are others. Anger and fear are two culprits when it comes to blocking the view of our Lord and Savior's amazing plans. Fear and anger reap destruction. They ruin friendships, destroy marriages, divide families and churches. Fear and anger can paralyze us and keep us from making the right choices.

**I sought the LORD, and he answered me; he delivered me from all my fears. Psalm 34:4**

Is there something going on in your life that causes you to be angry or afraid? Is there a big change you don't understand and don't like? Have you dug in your heels, resisted and complained without taking it to God in prayer and asking what His will is? Do you have the courage to follow God and ask for the strength to step out of your comfort zone? When we do, God does His best work.
It comes down to personal decisions. Some personal and tough questions! Do we want to be a part of His amazing plan? Are we willing to sacrifice, as He did for us, in order to further His kingdom? Are we willing to put ourselves aside and see what God has in mind? Are we willing to try something new for His kingdom's sake? It is not always comfortable, easy or natural to us, but it is an amazing feeling to be part of God's work. Is stepping out of your comfort zone and embracing change or offering forgiveness worth bringing others to Christ? Sometimes, that's what God calls us to do in order to bring others to Him.

Anyone who chooses to do the will of God will find out whether my teaching comes from God or whether I speak on my own. John 7:17

I pray that whatever anger or fear we hold onto today dissolves with each tear that falls and every word we lift up to our heavenly Father. This will ensure that Satan will not have his way with us. When I was growing up, before every overnight trip away from home, my mom would say, "Remember your morals, values and where you come from." In other words, do not get caught up in the moment and make a mistake you'll regret. Always remember, you are a child of God! Keep your eyes on the Light of the world. He is doing amazing things. Will you join Him?

to open their eyes and turn them from darkness to light, and from the power of Satan to God, so that they may receive forgiveness of sins and a place among those who are sanctified by faith in me. Acts 26:18

~~~~~~

### Monday – Find a word
Choose a word from the devotion or cited scriptures to reflect on for the week. Some examples: sovereign, righteous, almighty, full, uphold, future, hope, love, obedience. What is your word? _____
Search your Bible commentary. What verses use your word? List them here. Use your journal if you need additional space.
_____
_____

### Tuesday – Define
Choose one to two words to define and then reread the scriptures, replacing the word with the definition. How did it take your understanding to a new level?

### Wednesday – Translate
Choose two or three different Bible translations. Read the Monday verses (cited in the devotional or found in your study) in each translation. Now write them in your journal.

### Thursday – Go the Distance
Read the entire chapter of your favorite verse for the week.

### Friday – Prayer
Close your eyes and talk to God or write out your prayer in your journal.

## Week 35 ~ Transfer Station

It is the LORD your God you must follow, and him you must revere. Keep his commands and obey him; serve him and hold fast to him. Deuteronomy 13:4

On a recent trip to Paris with my mom, we had to learn to navigate the underground because neither of us had ever lived in a city with a metro system. The language barrier made things a little more challenging, but my mom is a master with her map and we were pros at getting around the city by the end of the week. Two of the most important things we learned were: 1) pause and consult the map and 2) some stops are "transfer stations" where you get off one line and onto another going in a different direction to reach your ultimate destination. Oh, and never keep your metro ticket with change, cell phones or keys. They destroy the strip on the back of the ticket and render it useless! This is not a travel guide, so back to my point!

I started thinking about all the stops in my life where I felt like I was sitting at a transfer station. I had a choice to make about the direction I was going, and I had the option of consulting the Master or deciding on my own. Looking back, I see clearly that each decision made in consultation with the Bible and the Lord in prayer ended in a destination that was much more appealing than the ones I arrived at on my own.

**Then he said to them all: "If anyone would come after me, he must deny himself and take up his cross daily and follow me." Luke 9:23**

Are you at a crossroads or transfer station? Is there a decision or action you've been struggling to make in your life? If you haven't already, I encourage you to take it to God and pick up your Bible. If you've been praying and God does not seem to be listening (I've been there), I encourage you to keep praying and seeking God's wisdom. God does not have to pause and take a breath, but *we* make much better decisions when we do!

Why would you ever complain, O Jacob, or, whine, Israel, saying, "God has lost track of me. He doesn't care what happens to me"? Don't you know anything? Haven't you been listening? God doesn't come and go. God lasts. He's Creator of all you can see or imagine. He doesn't get tired out, doesn't pause to catch his breath. And he knows everything, inside and out. He energizes those who get tired, gives fresh strength to dropouts. For even young people tire and drop out, young folk in their prime stumble and fall. But those who wait upon God get fresh strength. They spread their wings and soar like eagles. They run and don't get tired, they walk and don't lag behind. Isaiah 40:27 (The Message)

~~~~~~

## Monday – Find a word

Choose a word from the devotion or cited scriptures to reflect on for the week. Some examples: sovereign, righteous, almighty, full, uphold, future, hope, love, obedience. What is your word? _____

Search your Bible commentary. What verses use your word? List them here. Use your journal if you need additional space.

_____
_____
_____


## Tuesday – Define

Choose one to two words to define and then reread the scriptures, replacing the word with the definition. How did it take your understanding to a new level?

## Wednesday – Translate

Choose two or three different Bible translations. Read the Monday verses (cited in the devotional or found in your study) in each translation. Now write them in your journal.

## Thursday – Go the Distance

Read the entire chapter of your favorite verse for the week.

## Friday – Prayer

Close your eyes and talk to God or write out your prayer in your journal.

# Week 36 ~ Light

And God said, "Let there be light," and there was light. Genesis 1:3

We were recently out of town visiting family, and we all slept in the same room, chatting before we went to sleep. When I turned out the light, it was pitch dark. I knew I'd turned on a nightlight for the kids, but I could not see it. I got up to check, but in a few seconds my eyes adjusted and the room seemed to fill up with light. The nightlight was definitely casting the light, but my eyes needed time to adjust.

And God said, "Let there be lights in the expanse of the sky to separate the day from the night, and let them serve as signs to mark seasons and days and years," Genesis 1:14

As I lay there praying, I thanked God for His word – a light in this dark world that helps us put things in perspective. It teaches, it sheds light on life's challenges and it shows us how to deal with them. I am not saying it takes away the despair of losing a loved one, the heartbreak of broken vows or the tears of pain or that it instantly cures addiction or depression. But I am saying that it offers a hope – a healing – and a peace that nothing but God's light can give us. God is the Light of this world! He wants to be a radiant energy in your life, illuminating all that is good and the path you can follow. Allow Him into your life to ignite a fire in your soul that will guide you and light the path He intends for you to follow.

I have come into the world as a light, so that no one who believes in me should stay in darkness. John 12:46

~~~~~~

### Monday – Find a word

Choose a word from the devotion or cited scriptures to reflect on for the week. Some examples: sovereign, righteous, almighty, full, uphold, future, hope, love, obedience. What is your word? _____

Search your Bible commentary. What verses use your word? List them here. Use your journal if you need additional space.

_____
_____
_____
_____

### Tuesday – Define

Choose one to two words to define and then reread the scriptures, replacing the word with the definition. How did it take your understanding to a new level?

### Wednesday – Translate

Choose two or three different Bible translations. Read the Monday verses (cited in the devotional or found in your study) in each translation. Now write them in your journal.

### Thursday – Go the Distance

Read the entire chapter of your favorite verse for the week.

### Friday – Prayer

Close your eyes and talk to God or write out your prayer in your journal.

# Week 37 ~ Transition

My brother came to visit a few nights before school started for the year. He was discussing the ins and outs of second grade with my daughter and then turned to my son. "Are you in kindergarten this year?" he asked. "No, I am in transition!" my son exclaimed.

"Aren't we all?" my brother and I both said under our breath.
Are you in transition, too? It seems to be the case for most everyone in my family or circle of friends. Whether it's related to school, home, job, relationship, finances or family, transition is change and it can be difficult and strenuous emotionally, physically and spiritually.

**Like a will that takes effect when someone dies, the new covenant was put into action at Jesus' death. His death marked the transition from the old plan to the new one, canceling the old obligations and accompanying sins, and summoning the heirs to receive the eternal inheritance that was promised them. He brought together God and his people in this new way. Hebrews 9:16-17 (The Message)**

Sometimes the "old plan" is all we know, so when the "new plan" comes along we resist out of habit, fear or even anger. We've all heard the saying, "If there is one thing you can count on – it's change." Well, I would have to agree with that statement EXCEPT when it comes to our heavenly Father.

**As he preached he said, "The real action comes next: The star in this drama, to whom I'm a mere stagehand, will change your life. I'm baptizing you here in the river, turning your old life in for a kingdom life. His baptism – a holy baptism by the Holy Spirit – will change you from the inside out." Mark 1:7-8 (The Message)**

Our God has not changed and will not change. He remains the same "from everlasting to everlasting," but He will change us! He can change us in ways we'd never imagine. Glorious peace, comfort, compassion, forgiveness and more – for you, for me, for anyone who accepts it. Go for it! Start your transition. Let God into your life and allow Him to change you "from the inside out."

Before the mountains were born or you brought forth the earth and the world, from everlasting to everlasting you are God. Psalm 90:2

~~~~~~

### Monday – Find a word
Choose a word from the devotion or cited scriptures to reflect on for the week. Some examples: sovereign, righteous, almighty, full, uphold, future, hope, love, obedience. What is your word? _____

Search your Bible commentary. What verses use your word? List them here. Use your journal if you need additional space.

_____
_____
_____
_____

### Tuesday – Define
Choose one to two words to define and then reread the scriptures, replacing the word with the definition. How did it take your understanding to a new level?

### Wednesday – Translate
Choose two or three different Bible translations. Read the Monday verses (cited in the devotional or found in your study) in each translation. Now write them in your journal.

### Thursday – Go the Distance
Read the entire chapter of your favorite verse for the week.

### Friday – Prayer
Close your eyes and talk to God or write out your prayer in your journal.

# Week 38 ~ Run

A friend and her young daughter came over recently for a visit. At the end of the visit, when we announced to the children it was time to go, they all fled upstairs and hid away in the secret hideout. It was cute at first but, as it continued, we began to lose our patience.

One day long ago, God's Word came to Jonah, Amittai's son: "Up on your feet and on your way to the big city of Nineveh! Preach to them. They're in a bad way and I can't ignore it any longer." But Jonah got up and went the other direction to Tarshish, running away from God. Jonah 1:1-3

I can relate to Jonah. Before I published my first book, *The Whisper of God*, I was scared and, to be honest, I was more scared of success than failure. If you fail, you can say you tried and it didn't work out. If you are successful, it means change. I prayed, waited and gave God many opportunities to lead me in a different direction – a direction that meant not publishing my devotional. He persisted and, thankfully, this time I was too scared to run from Him. I chose to run toward Him. I would love to say that the decision came strictly from my obedience, but remembering and learning from the past "whale swallowing" moments in my life helped tremendously!

If we run from the Lord, we are giving up so many opportunities in our lives. Things we never could have imagined become reality when we allow Him in and follow His lead. Talk about scared! It scares me to think what could have happened if I hadn't followed God's nudge to lead a high school girls' Bible study, marriage seminar, small group or Wednesday morning Bible study in my home. All those interactions, relationships, opportunities to share and grow in Christ would have been lost if I had run away.

But be very careful to keep the commandment and the law that Moses the servant of the LORD gave you: to love the LORD your God, to walk in all his ways, to obey his commands, to hold fast to him and to serve him with all your heart and all your soul. Joshua 22:5

Are you trying to run away from something that God has placed on your heart? We run from things for all different reasons, but I am living proof that if it is God's plan and you are obedient, He will provide and give you all you need to succeed.

So you can run, but make sure you are running in the right direction!
**But you, Timothy, man of God: Run for your life from all this. Pursue a righteous life – a life of wonder, faith, love, steadiness, courtesy. Run hard and fast in the faith. Seize the eternal life, the life you were called to, the life you so fervently embraced in the presence of so many witnesses. 1 Timothy 6:11 (The Message)**

~~~~~~

### Monday – Find a word
Choose a word from the devotion or cited scriptures to reflect on for the week. Some examples: sovereign, righteous, almighty, full, uphold, future, hope, love, obedience. What is your word? _____

Search your Bible commentary. What verses use your word? List them here. Use your journal if you need additional space.
_____
_____
_____

### Tuesday – Define
Choose one to two words to define and then reread the scriptures, replacing the word with the definition. How did it take your understanding to a new level?

### Wednesday – Translate
Choose two or three different Bible translations. Read the Monday verses (cited in the devotional or found in your study) in each translation. Now write them in your journal.

### Thursday – Go the Distance
Read the entire chapter of your favorite verse for the week.

### Friday – Prayer
Close your eyes and talk to God or write out your prayer in your journal.

# Week 39 ~ Trust or Denial?

"Mommy, can cockroaches tickle me?" my son asked on the way to visit a friend. I laughed and laughed at this question and wondered how it'd come up in his mind. It made my morning. This really has nothing to do with today's devotion other than to remind us to take more time to listen, laugh and relax. It's good for the heart!

Sometimes, people look at me and wonder how I can remain balanced and at peace in during times of extreme stress or hardship and it makes me start to question myself. Doubt enters my mind, and I wonder if my calm and trusting heart is due more to denial than my trust in God. I know these doubts are only Satan's way of creeping into my heart and trying to steal away the trust and truth the Lord offers me.

**Guard your heart more than anything else, because the source of your life flows from it. Proverbs 4:23 (God's Word Translation)**
So our heart is the **"wellspring of life"** (Proverbs 4:23 NIV), **"where life starts"** (The Message) and **"determines the course of your life"** (NLT). The condition of our heart determines the course of our life. That's a powerful statement. What is the condition of your heart? Have you checked on it lately?

God has come to light this dark world, to give us hope, new life, peace and redemption. He wants His light to flow out of our hearts and into those around us for His glory. I pray we will all guard our hearts so that seeds of doubt cannot enter and grow into fear, distrust and resentment. Trust or denial? I choose TRUST!

This is the crisis we're in: God-light streamed into the world, but men and women everywhere ran for the darkness. They went for the darkness because they were not really interested in pleasing God. Everyone who makes a practice of doing evil, addicted to denial and illusion, hates God-light and won't come near it, fearing a painful exposure. But anyone working and living in truth and reality welcomes God-light so the work can be seen for the God-work it is. John 3:19 (The Message)

~~~~~~

### Monday – Find a word
Choose a word from the devotion or cited scriptures to reflect on for the week. Some examples: sovereign, righteous, almighty, full, uphold, future, hope, love, obedience. What is your word? _____

Search your Bible commentary. What verses use your word? List them here. Use your journal if you need additional space.

_____
_____
_____
_____

### Tuesday – Define
Choose one to two words to define and then reread the scriptures, replacing the word with the definition. How did it take your understanding to a new level?

### Wednesday – Translate
Choose two or three different Bible translations. Read the Monday verses (cited in the devotional or found in your study) in each translation. Now write them in your journal.

### Thursday – Go the Distance
Read the entire chapter of your favorite verse for the week.

### Friday – Prayer
Close your eyes and talk to God or write out your prayer in your journal.

# Week 40 ~ Destruction

**For man's anger does not bring about the righteous life that God desires. James 1:20**

When I was in elementary school, we had a wonderful babysitter named Cheryl. She always played with us, brought us treats and was more like a family member than a sitter. One day she brought me an adorable ceramic kitten that she had painted. I treasured it not only because she had given it to me, but because I adored anything to do with cats or kittens when I was younger.

Several weeks later, I got mad at my mom. She probably wanted me to clean my room, do my homework or something that seemed horrible at the time. I remember sitting on my bed and making the decision to tear all the paint off the kitten to get back at my mom. It felt like a good idea at the time and I reveled in every piece I tore off. Later, when my mom entered the room and saw what I had done, all I could do was cry. Although my intention was to hurt my mom, destroying the kitten had only hurt me.

**If you, God, kept records on wrongdoings, who would stand a chance? As it turns out, forgiveness is your habit, and that's why you're worshiped. Psalm 130:3**

It was an early lesson, but it had an impact on me. In fact, all the emotions of sadness, remorse and guilt rise as I tell the story. Anger, bitterness, revenge and destruction are tied up into one messy package. These emotions can lead to the destruction of a friendship, marriage, job, ministry and ultimately your relationship with Christ.

**Refrain from anger and turn from wrath; do not fret – it leads only to evil. Psalm 37:8**

God created us. He knows us from the inside out and expects us to experience all of these emotions. The problem occurs when these emotions cause us to sin – when we decide to take revenge for ourselves or hold onto anger that eats away at our own heart and no one else.

If these emotions have taken hold in your heart, I pray God reveals them to you and that you can hand them over to Him in exchange for a forgiving and peaceful heart.

**In your anger do not sin; when you are on your beds, search your hearts and be silent. Psalm 4:4**

~~~~~~

### Monday – Find a word
Choose a word from the devotion or cited scriptures to reflect on for the week. Some examples: sovereign, righteous, almighty, full, uphold, future, hope, love, obedience. What is your word? _____

Search your Bible commentary. What verses use your word? List them here. Use your journal if you need additional space.
_____
_____
_____

### Tuesday – Define
Choose one to two words to define and then reread the scriptures, replacing the word with the definition. How did it take your understanding to a new level?

### Wednesday – Translate
Choose two or three different Bible translations. Read the Monday verses (cited in the devotional or found in your study) in each translation. Now write them in your journal.

### Thursday – Go the Distance
Read the entire chapter of your favorite verse for the week.

### Friday – Prayer
Close your eyes and talk to God or write out your prayer in your journal.

# Week 41 ~ But . . .

You, therefore, have no excuse, you who pass judgment on someone else, for at whatever point you judge the other, you are condemning yourself, because you who pass judgment do the same things. Romans 2:1

B-u-t. These three letters can drive me absolutely nutty! It's like a whole argument or excuse tied up in one tiny word. "But, Mommy, they took my toy." "But, Mommy, they hit me first, they said I was mean, they told me I could not be their friend anymore." "But, but, but!" It's amazing how my children can use that one word to justify hitting someone, name calling, toy snatching or breaking some other rule we've established in our home. One day I'd had enough of the "buts" and pulled out the "but, nothing!" retort. It was inevitable, I know, but I try not to use those traditional "mom" lines too often.

Later, as I reflected on the day, I realized how often I am guilty of the "but" excuse. Not just with others, but with God. Even as adults, we try to justify and explain actions and thoughts that we know do not reflect the kingdom of God. "But, she started a rumor about me. But, he treated me unfairly. But, she lied to me. But, they promised. They betrayed my trust. But, I deserve it after all I did for them." Do any of those statements sound familiar?

Do not seek revenge or bear a grudge against one of your people, but love your neighbor as yourself. I am the LORD. Leviticus 19:18

"But" is just a disclaimer that means, "I am accountable unless this happens, except for when, contrary to what you think." There are no buts with God, no excuses. He calls us to forgive, to obey, to trust and to treat others as more important than ourselves. Ugh! This is not always easy. In fact, a lot of times it seems almost impossible. The only way it's possible is with the power, strength and love of the Holy Spirit.

Today I pray that the Lord will remove the "buts" and excuses from our hearts and fill us with forgiveness, gratitude, acceptance and love for ourselves and for those around us.

"But, nothing!" I couldn't resist saying it one more time.

**Be devoted to one another in brotherly love. Honor one another above yourselves.
Romans 12:1**

~~~~~~

### Monday – Find a word

Choose a word from the devotion or cited scriptures to reflect on for the week. Some examples: sovereign, righteous, almighty, full, uphold, future, hope, love, obedience. What is your word? _____

Search your Bible commentary. What verses use your word? List them here. Use your journal if you need additional space.

_____
_____
_____
_____

### Tuesday – Define

Choose one to two words to define and then reread the scriptures, replacing the word with the definition. How did it take your understanding to a new level?

### Wednesday – Translate

Choose two or three different Bible translations. Read the Monday verses (cited in the devotional or found in your study) in each translation. Now write them in your journal.

### Thursday – Go the Distance

Read the entire chapter of your favorite verse for the week.

### Friday – Prayer

Close your eyes and talk to God or write out your prayer in your journal.

# Week 42 ~ Shine

In the beginning was the Word, and the Word was with God, and the Word was God. He was in the beginning with God. All things were made through him, and without him was not any thing made that was made. In him was life, and the life was the light of men. The light shines in the darkness, and the darkness has not overcome it. John 1:1-5

You know those days or weeks when you find yourself worn out, and good news seems like a train that left the station weeks ago and has yet to return? As I was driving the kids to school one morning, I was recounting (in my head) all the discouraging things going on in my life and in the lives of my loved ones. So many times the **"worries of this life, the deceitfulness of wealth and the desires for other things come in and choke the word, making it unfruitful."** Mark 4:19

As we drove to the top of a hill on Wade Avenue, I saw a rainbow in the sky. It was a sunny morning with just a few clouds heading out after an overnight storm. The rays from the sunrise must have been hitting the clouds just right, and there it appeared. My thoughts immediately turned from sadness to praise and I felt peace overcome me.

Like the appearance of a rainbow in the clouds on a rainy day, so was the radiance around him. This was the appearance of the likeness of the glory of the LORD. When I saw it, I fell facedown, and I heard the voice of one speaking. Ezekiel 1:28

God is our light on those dark days and He is the Light that always shines in the darkness. Our God is so faithful and so tender. That rainbow was a beautiful reminder of His promises. Not just the promise that **"never again will the waters become a flood to destroy all life,"** Genesis 9:15 but a promise of His love for us. He is always with us. He walks with us through fiery trials, He celebrates with us, He carries us when we cannot take another step, He feels our pain and He counts our tears.

The next time clouds overtake you, look to the sky. Look to God and rely on His promises to carry you through. He is there for you and His light will always **shine through the darkness. John 1:5**

~~~~~~

### Monday – Find a word

Choose a word from the devotion or cited scriptures to reflect on for the week. Some examples: sovereign, righteous, almighty, full, uphold, future, hope, love, obedience. What is your word? _____

Search your Bible commentary. What verses use your word? List them here. Use your journal if you need additional space.

_____
_____
_____
_____

### Tuesday – Define

Choose one to two words to define and then reread the scriptures, replacing the word with the definition. How did it take your understanding to a new level?

### Wednesday – Translate

Choose two or three different Bible translations. Read the Monday verses (cited in the devotional or found in your study) in each translation. Now write them in your journal.

### Thursday – Go the Distance

Read the entire chapter of your favorite verse for the week.

### Friday – Prayer

Close your eyes and talk to God or write out your prayer in your journal.

# Week 43 ~ Persist

**May the Lord direct your hearts into God's love and Christ's perseverance.
2 Thessalonians 3:5**

My daughter and I started playing a new game. She takes her dictionary, flips to a random page and picks the oddest word she sees there. Then, it's my turn. Once I've found my word, we compare the two and decide whose is strangest. It's been fun and I've actually learned a lot of new words.

One day, we happened upon the word perseverance. The dictionary defines perseverance as a "continued steady belief or efforts, withstanding discouragement or difficulty; persistence." I knew the definition included not giving up, even under difficult circumstances, but I'd never considered the part about "continued steady belief or effort." There are many scripture references to perseverance and endurance in the Bible. God knew how much encouragement we would need in this earthly life – with its challenges, disappointments, fears and disasters – to maintain a steady belief in Him and His word.

**Because you know that the testing of your faith develops perseverance. Perseverance must finish its work so that you may be mature and complete, not lacking anything. If any of you lacks wisdom, he should ask God, who gives generously to all without finding fault, and it will be given to him. James 1:3-5**

God has blessed me with an amazing group of friends. We've been through so much together. In fact, sometimes we pray God will give us a break from all the "faith building" activities He's had us endure. I am not exaggerating when I say we've endured adultery, divorce, financial difficulties, a friend's death, terminally ill children, betrayal by family members and more. Together, we've grown in faith and we are constantly amazed and grateful. I am grateful for friends, for prayer warriors, for God's faithfulness and for the fact that all we've endured is not wasted or forgotten. Instead, our trials and experiences shape us in our friendships, marriages, lives and, most importantly, they strengthen us in our relationship with Christ.

When faced with trials, we have a choice. We can choose misery, distrust, anger, bitterness, sadness, and we can turn away from the Lord. As for my friends and me, we choose hope, character and love. We choose the Lord! What do you choose?

Not only so, but we also rejoice in our sufferings, because we know that suffering produces perseverance; perseverance, character; and character, hope. And hope does not disappoint us, because God has poured out his love into our hearts by the Holy Spirit, whom he has given us. Romans 3:3-5

~~~~~~

### Monday – Find a word
Choose a word from the devotion or cited scriptures to reflect on for the week. Some examples: sovereign, righteous, almighty, full, uphold, future, hope, love, obedience. What is your word? _____

Search your Bible commentary. What verses use your word? List them here. Use your journal if you need additional space.

_____
_____
_____


### Tuesday – Define
Choose one to two words to define and then reread the scriptures, replacing the word with the definition. How did it take your understanding to a new level?

### Wednesday – Translate
Choose two or three different Bible translations. Read the Monday verses (cited in the devotional or found in your study) in each translation. Now write them in your journal.

### Thursday – Go the Distance
Read the entire chapter of your favorite verse for the week.

### Friday – Prayer
Close your eyes and talk to God or write out your prayer in your journal.

# Week 44 ~ Unsearchable

Call to me and I will answer you and tell you great and unsearchable things you do not know. Jeremiah 33:3

I had just answered my son's 73rd question of the day, and it was only one o'clock in the afternoon. I try to be patient and answer each question with as much thought and energy as the first one of the day, but it gets difficult. I was a little frustrated and gave him a quick, "Yes!" to which he replied, "Mommy, you know why I ask you lots of questions? You are the mom and you know everything. I am just a kid. It's your job to teach me." Well, what can you say to that?

Our Lord and Savior promises to tell us wondrous and amazing things we could never imagine. The NIV translation (Jeremiah 33:3) uses the word "unsearchable." Unsearchable is defined as "not searchable; not lending itself to research or exploration; not to be understood by searching; hidden; unfathomable; mysterious: the unsearchable ways of the universe."

Who doesn't like to know hidden, secret or mysterious things? God is offering each of us the opportunity to know "great and unsearchable things." Things we will never know unless we ask Him to reveal them to us.

**Although I am less than the least of all God's people, this grace was given me: to preach to the Gentiles the unsearchable riches of Christ, Ephesians 3:8**

The Bible is the perfect map for life's adventure/journey. It's God's word – spoken to you and to me. He is reaching out and wants us to call to Him so that He can reveal "marvelous and wondrous" things to us. We don't need a secret map, a special key, lots of money or anything else. We need only to call to Him. When He answers, will you be listening?

> Call to me and I will answer you. I'll tell you marvelous and wondrous things that you could never figure out on your own. – Jeremiah 33:3 (The Message)

~~~~~~

### Monday – Find a word

Choose a word from the devotion or cited scriptures to reflect on for the week. Some examples: sovereign, righteous, almighty, full, uphold, future, hope, love, obedience. What is your word? _____

Search your Bible commentary. What verses use your word? List them here. Use your journal if you need additional space.

_____
_____
_____
_____

### Tuesday – Define

Choose one to two words to define and then reread the scriptures, replacing the word with the definition. How did it take your understanding to a new level?

### Wednesday – Translate

Choose two or three different Bible translations. Read the Monday verses (cited in the devotional or found in your study) in each translation. Now write them in your journal.

### Thursday – Go the Distance

Read the entire chapter of your favorite verse for the week.

### Friday – Prayer

Close your eyes and talk to God or write out your prayer in your journal.

## Week 45 ~ In This World

My son's favorite question to ask is, "Mommy, are there . . . (superheroes, bad guys, sharks, etc.) in this world?" I get a couple of those questions each day. He's trying to figure out if everything he reads, sees on television or hears is real "in this world."

Most recently I found myself trying to explain that there are bad guys in this world, but they don't have superpowers. I'm not sure how it came out, and I don't even remember what I said, but he seemed to get it. Or maybe I just confused him so much he dropped the subject. There are many wonderful things in this world – and just as many things that are not wonderful. As Christians, how do we keep ourselves from getting confused about what is true and what is not? How do we make decisions that will store up treasures in Heaven instead of temporary wealth in this world?

**Do not store up for yourselves treasures on earth, where moth and rust destroy, and where thieves break in and steal. Matthew 6:19**

Jesus looked him hard in the eye – and loved him! He said, "There's one thing left: Go sell whatever you own and give it to the poor. All your wealth will then be heavenly wealth. And come follow me." Mark 10:21

We MUST read God's written word, study it, pray, soak in God's presence and worship Him. All of these practices have led me to a closer relationship with my heavenly Father. My friends and I often ponder this: "How do those who don't know Christ make it through this world and the tragedies, pain, heartache, sickness, despair?" Honestly, I don't think they do make it. I believe they turn to money, alcohol, work, drugs, pornography, exercise or anything else. They focus on other things to numb the pain, loss and loneliness they feel. My favorite song (I call it my life theme song) is by Mandisa. It's called *Only The World*. She says it best in these lyrics:

*"Cause it's only the world I'm living in, It's only the day I've been given. There ain't a way I'm giving in cause it's only the world.*

*I know the best is still yet to come cause even when my deeds in the world are done. It's gonna be so much more than only the world to me."*

**He will wipe every tear from their eyes. There will be no more death or mourning or crying or pain, for the old order of things has passed away. He who was seated on the throne said, "I am making everything new!" Then he said, "Write this down, for these words are trustworthy and true." Revelation 21:4-5**

~~~~~~

### Monday – Find a word
Choose a word from the devotion or cited scriptures to reflect on for the week. Some examples: sovereign, righteous, almighty, full, uphold, future, hope, love, obedience. What is your word? _____

Search your Bible commentary. What verses use your word? List them here. Use your journal if you need additional space.

_____
_____
_____
_____

### Tuesday – Define
Choose one to two words to define and then reread the scriptures, replacing the word with the definition. How did it take your understanding to a new level?

### Wednesday – Translate
Choose two or three different Bible translations. Read the Monday verses (cited in the devotional or found in your study) in each translation. Now write them in your journal.

### Thursday – Go the Distance
Read the entire chapter of your favorite verse for the week.

### Friday – Prayer
Close your eyes and talk to God or write out your prayer in your journal.

# Week 46 ~ "They" Say...

Don't let anyone look down on you because you are young, but set an example for the believers in speech, in life, in love, in faith and in purity. 1 Timothy 4:12

I couldn't help but overhear the conversation in the checkout line. "You know what they say," the woman declared, trying to prove her point to a friend. "No, what?" her friend asked, as if she was waiting for the million-dollar lottery number. I couldn't help but smile to myself. I desperately wanted to ask her, "Do you know who 'they' are?"

"They" say a lot don't they?! Who are "they" anyway? I think about that when I hear or use "they say" as a defense. We need to be careful that we don't get caught up in worrying about what "they" say more than what Jesus says. Too often we resort to the news, friends, celebrities or others to help shape our morals, values, decisions or actions. All the direction and guidance we need is in God's written word.

In the Sermon on the Mount, Jesus points out several "they said" examples and corrects us on the truth. He tells us what "we have heard" and directs us back to His word.

You have heard that it was said, "Eye for eye, and tooth for tooth." But I tell you, Do not resist an evil person. If someone strikes you on the right cheek, turn to him the other also. Matthew 5:38-39

You have heard that it was said, "Do not commit adultery." But I tell you that anyone who looks at a woman lustfully has already committed adultery with her in his heart. Matthew 5:27-28

You have heard that it was said, "Love your neighbor and hate your enemy." But I tell you: Love your enemies and pray for those who persecute you, Matthew 5:43-44

No matter how young, old, rich or poor we might be, we can never go wrong when we are setting an example of Christ to others around us. To do this you must study His word, know His ways, His truth and what "He" has to say.

~~~~~~

### Monday – Find a word
Choose a word from the devotion or cited scriptures to reflect on for the week. Some examples: sovereign, righteous, almighty, full, uphold, future, hope, love, obedience. What is your word? _____

Search your Bible commentary. What verses use your word? List them here. Use your journal if you need additional space.

_____
_____
_____
_____

### Tuesday – Define
Choose one to two words to define and then reread the scriptures, replacing the word with the definition. How did it take your understanding to a new level?

### Wednesday – Translate
Choose two or three different Bible translations. Read the Monday verses (cited in the devotional or found in your study) in each translation. Now write them in your journal.

### Thursday – Go the Distance
Read the entire chapter of your favorite verse for the week.

### Friday – Prayer
Close your eyes and talk to God or write out your prayer in your journal.

# Week 47 ~ Mire

I waited patiently for the LORD; he turned to me and heard my cry. He lifted me out of the slimy pit, out of the mud and mire; he set my feet on a rock and gave me a firm place to stand. Psalm 40:1-2

As we drove along one day and sang a great song about Psalm 40:1-2, my daughter asked, "What is mire, anyway?" "Wet and soggy mud," I said. "Yuck, that sounds terrible," she replied.

Yes, as adults, we know exactly how ugly, soggy, messy and dismal life's circumstances can be. Right now, I have a list of prayer requests that range from restoring a marriage to healing a 7-year-old child with terminal cancer. We know how the mud and mire of life can get thick and we can get stuck in it. Sometimes we're unable to find our way out or we lack the strength and faith to fight our way out.

**Turn your ear to me, come quickly to my rescue; be my rock of refuge, a strong fortress to save me. Psalm 31:2**

So often we search for an answer, look for a way out, grasp at anything in hope that this time we'll be successful – that we'll be able to pull ourselves out of the mire. I have good news and bad news: We are not capable of doing it. We cannot pull ourselves out. But God can and He will, if we ask and allow Him to do it for us.

The problem is – unlike this world that forces ideas, temptations and moral codes on us – God will not force Himself on us. He wants us to choose Him. To choose His promises and His truth. It seems so easy it doesn't seem real, but it is! He is real! After telling me about a difficult situation in her life, a friend said, "Every day I get up and I <u>choose</u> trust!" Every part of this world is pulling her back into the mire, but she gets up and chooses God.

We have to choose Him! He desperately wants us to grab the hand He has extended to pull us out of the mire and place us on solid ground. But we have to choose Him. We have to choose to take His hand. Will you accept His hand and step out of the mire and onto the Rock?

**The LORD lives! Praise be to my Rock! Exalted be God, the Rock, my Savior! 2 Samuel 22:47**

~~~~~~

### Monday – Find a word
Choose a word from the devotion or cited scriptures to reflect on for the week. Some examples: sovereign, righteous, almighty, full, uphold, future, hope, love, obedience. What is your word? _____

Search your Bible commentary. What verses use your word? List them here. Use your journal if you need additional space.

_____
_____
_____

### Tuesday – Define
Choose one to two words to define and then reread the scriptures, replacing the word with the definition. How did it take your understanding to a new level?

### Wednesday – Translate
Choose two or three different Bible translations. Read the Monday verses (cited in the devotional or found in your study) in each translation. Now write them in your journal.

### Thursday – Go the Distance
Read the entire chapter of your favorite verse for the week.

### Friday – Prayer
Close your eyes and talk to God or write out your prayer in your journal.

# Week 48 ~ The Edge

I was spending the morning at home, cooking for a friend who'd recently given birth. I found myself uncomfortable with so much time on my hands as I waited for the meal to cook. It's seldom that I have any free time. I prayed, "God, show me how you want me to spend my time this morning." Without a pause, I heard my heart call out, "Spend it with Me!" Of course. As I walked down the hallway toward my Bible and looked out the front door, I saw a newspaper hung up in the thorns of our rose bushes. We don't even subscribe to the newspaper. There I was, on my way to the Bible, and within seconds the world had distracted me. I found myself starting to go out to get the paper. "I never get to just sit and read the newspaper," I thought as I tried to justify the tempting change of plans. Surely, if "the newspaper" had been my choice, I would've gotten tangled up in more than the thorns on the rose bush.

You must be thinking, "Big deal if you chose the newspaper. That won't get you into any trouble." Satan wants us to believe that. But it occurred to me that most sin starts small. If we continue to make the same bad choice, it becomes habit, and eventually we're so far along it becomes easier to stay on that path than get back on the right one.

**Staying with it – that's what God requires. Stay with it to the end. You won't be sorry, and you'll be saved. All during this time, the good news – the Message of the kingdom—will be preached all over the world, a witness staked out in every country. And then the end will come. Matthew 24:13 (The Message)**

The more I choose television and computer over Bible study, the easier it gets to leave God behind. The more we tell a little lie here and there, the easier it gets the next time. The more time we spend with someone of the opposite sex, instead of our spouse, the likelier we are to fall victim to adultery. We must be careful to avoid the mistaken belief that a lie is a lesser sin than adultery. We rank sins in our minds, but God does not rank our sins.

**When he came back to his disciples, he found them sound asleep. He said to Peter, "Can't you stick it out with me a single hour?**

Stay alert; be in prayer so you don't wander into temptation without even knowing you're in danger. There is a part of you that is eager, ready for anything in God. But there's another part that's as lazy as an old dog sleeping by the fire."
Matthew 26:40

We are all on the edge in some area of our lives. What area of your life needs a little more margin? When we continually choose the world over our Lord and Savior, we become vulnerable to the sins of this world. We have to choose God. We have to choose to stay in His word so that we can stay in His will. God does not warn us about danger to be controlling or to keep us from having fun. Like most parents, He teaches and guides us through His word in hopes of keeping us from pain, sadness and destruction.

~~~~~~

### Monday – Find a word
Choose a word from the devotion or cited scriptures to reflect on for the week. Some examples: sovereign, righteous, almighty, full, uphold, future, hope, love, obedience. What is your word? _____

Search your Bible commentary. What verses use your word? List them here. Use your journal if you need additional space.

_____
_____
_____

### Tuesday – Define
Choose one to two words to define and then reread the scriptures, replacing the word with the definition. How did it take your understanding to a new level?

### Wednesday – Translate
Choose two or three different Bible translations. Read the Monday verses (cited in the devotional or found in your study) in each translation. Now write them in your journal.

### Thursday – Go the Distance
Read the entire chapter of your favorite verse for the week.

### Friday – Prayer
Close your eyes and talk to God or write out your prayer in your journal.

## Week 49 ~Training

My son and I were spending some time in the school library and found a book on insects. A large beetle with two big pincers caught his eye. As we began to read, we discovered that the male beetle is very weak, so you don't have to worry about him hurting you. But you should worry about the female because she's much stronger. I could tell he was having a tough time digesting this beetle fact, and I must not have done a good job explaining how it's possible for a girl to be stronger than a boy. Later that evening, out of the blue, he said, "Mommy, when I grow up I want to be a beetle trainer so I can teach all the boy beetles to be as strong as the girl beetles!"

I giggled, but it made me think about the responsibility we have as Christians. Should we place a high priority on teaching and training others in Christ so they can grow stronger in their relationship with Him? We all have spiritual gifts. Not all of us can teach Bible study, give speeches and sermons or graduate from divinity school. Thankfully we don't have to do all or any of these things. But we can choose to live as an example so that we teach and share God with others around us.

**Now you are the body of Christ, and each one of you is a part of it. And in the church God has appointed first of all apostles, second prophets, third teachers, then workers of miracles, also those having gifts of healing, those able to help others, those with gifts of administration, and those speaking in different kinds of tongues. Are all apostles? Are all prophets? Are all teachers? Do all work miracles? 1 Corinthians 12:27**

Have you thought about what you're teaching others each day? Have you considered what your spiritual gifts are and how you could put them to use for God's glory? It's not always easy to use your gifts, and it can certainly take you out of your comfort zone. When I open my heart to the Holy Spirit, there is never a day I go before God that I'm not humbled and in awe of all He's enabled me to do. I pray the same for you.

You then, my son, be strong in the grace that is in Christ Jesus. And the things you have heard me say in the presence of many witnesses entrust to reliable men who will also be qualified to teach others. 2 Timothy 2:1-2

~~~~~~

### Monday – Find a word
Choose a word from the devotion or cited scriptures to reflect on for the week. Some examples: sovereign, righteous, almighty, full, uphold, future, hope, love, obedience. What is your word? _____

Search your Bible commentary. What verses use your word? List them here. Use your journal if you need additional space.

_____
_____
_____
_____

### Tuesday – Define
Choose one to two words to define and then reread the scriptures, replacing the word with the definition. How did it take your understanding to a new level?

### Wednesday – Translate
Choose two or three different Bible translations. Read the Monday verses (cited in the devotional or found in your study) in each translation. Now write them in your journal.

### Thursday – Go the Distance
Read the entire chapter of your favorite verse for the week.

### Friday – Prayer
Close your eyes and talk to God or write out your prayer in your journal.

# Week 50 ~ Raw

Your best friend breaks your confidence, your child goes off to school, you receive the family phone call you've been dreading, your career has been downsized, your husband breaks his marriage vows. When distressing things happen, we often feel numb. The reality of the situation has to sink in. But with time, we may also begin to feel raw, as if we've been unnaturally or painfully exposed. The way we treat an agonizing emotional wound is important to proper healing.

but the crowds learned about it and followed him. He welcomed them and spoke to them about the kingdom of God, and healed those who needed healing. Luke 9:11

Pain from these raw wounds can take over our life if we don't allow God into our heart to begin the healing process. This can be difficult when we don't understand why He would allow something hurtful to happen to us. We want to ignore or blame Him. Like you, I've experienced painful things in my life. After time passes, God has revealed many lessons through the hurt. I now refuse to waste any of the suffering endured by my friends or myself. I have promised the Lord and those I love that I will cling to the lessons learned from these experiences. I will not forget them, the pain or the good that eventually arises from difficult situations. We must defeat the lies of Satan. He will tell us we deserved pain. But with God's shield, we can experience His healing, His grace and His truth.

All praise to the God and Father of our Master, Jesus the Messiah! Father of all mercy! God of all healing counsel! He comes alongside us when we go through hard times, and before you know it, he brings us alongside someone else who is going through hard times so that we can be there for that person just as God was there for us. We have plenty of hard times that come from following the Messiah, but no more so than the good times of his healing comfort—we get a full measure of that, too. 2 Corinthians 1:3-5 (The Message)

~~~~~~

### Monday – Find a word

Choose a word from the devotion or cited scriptures to reflect on for the week. Some examples: sovereign, righteous, almighty, full, uphold, future, hope, love, obedience. What is your word? _____

Search your Bible commentary. What verses use your word? List them here. Use your journal if you need additional space.

_____
_____
_____
_____

### Tuesday – Define

Choose one to two words to define and then reread the scriptures, replacing the word with the definition. How did it take your understanding to a new level?

### Wednesday – Translate

Choose two or three different Bible translations. Read the Monday verses (cited in the devotional or found in your study) in each translation. Now write them in your journal.

### Thursday – Go the Distance

Read the entire chapter of your favorite verse for the week.

### Friday – Prayer

Close your eyes and talk to God or write out your prayer in your journal.

## Week 51 ~ The Race

In an effort to get the kids into bed after a long evening, I told them I'd give a prize to the first one to put on pajamas, brush teeth and get under the covers. My daughter quickly began tackling the challenge. My son, however, melted into a puddle on the bathroom floor, crying, "Mommy, I cannot do it. I cannot do all that. Emma always wins and I always lose."

My son was so discouraged from just listening to the challenge that he didn't try. He was convinced, based on past experience, that he would not be able to compete and finish before his sister.

**Do you not know that in a race all the runners run, but only one gets the prize? Run in such a way as to get the prize. Everyone who competes in the games goes into strict training. They do it to get a crown that will not last; but we do it to get a crown that will last forever. Therefore I do not run like a man running aimlessly; I do not fight like a man beating the air. No, I beat my body and make it my slave so that after I have preached to others, I myself will not be disqualified for the prize. 1 Corinthians 9:24-27**

For years, I worried about not living or praying the right way – the Christian way. All the rules, the commandments, the guidelines and expectations felt too overwhelming. I knew I could never do all those things well enough or consistently enough to please God, much less to be used for His purpose. I felt defeated and inadequate, and my walk with Christ suffered because of it.

However, through God's grace and years of Bible study, Christian mentors and prayer, my eyes have been opened to the truth – His Truth! God does not expect perfection from us. He knows we cannot win the race, at least not without Him. He wants us to come to Him messy, confused and uncertain, but with a desire to seek Him and learn His ways.

Does that lift a 1,000-pound weight off your shoulders like it does mine? Grace is not earned through perfect prayer, adherence to every commandment, perfect church attendance, gifts to charity or other actions. Grace is what we do not deserve and, thankfully, what God has already given to us.

Are you trying to earn God's grace? It cannot be done, my friend. It's like begging to be released from prison when the door's been open all along and you just had to walk through it. God is pleased with you! Be bold in believing that truth so that you can go out and share His truth with others.

~~~~~~

### Monday – Find a word
Choose a word from the devotion or cited scriptures to reflect on for the week. Some examples: sovereign, righteous, almighty, full, uphold, future, hope, love, obedience. What is your word? _____

Search your Bible commentary. What verses use your word? List them here. Use your journal if you need additional space.

_____
_____
_____

### Tuesday – Define
Choose one to two words to define and then reread the scriptures, replacing the word with the definition. How did it take your understanding to a new level?

### Wednesday – Translate
Choose two or three different Bible translations. Read the Monday verses (cited in the devotional or found in your study) in each translation. Now write them in your journal.

### Thursday – Go the Distance
Read the entire chapter of your favorite verse for the week.

### Friday – Prayer
Close your eyes and talk to God or write out your prayer in your journal.

# Week 52 ~ Not Now!

One morning, my daughter set up a nail salon in her bedroom. She had everything from business cards to bowls of warm water. When she asked her younger brother if he'd come to get his nails done, he responded firmly, "No, I am a boy." The second time she pleaded and he said, "Emma, I can't. I have to go fight crime."

I laughed until I thought about all the excuses I've used to get out of something God had nudged me to do. How many times have we felt God tugging at our hearts to do something and responded quickly with, "I can't do that." Then, as He's continued to pursue us, we've made up excuses – and they've seemed so legitimate. I don't have time, they might think I'm crazy, they won't listen to me anyway so why bother, it's out of my way, it's not on my schedule for the day. We just reason ourselves out of it.

**The word of the LORD came to Jonah son of Amittai: "Go to the great city of Nineveh and preach against it, because its wickedness has come up before me."But Jonah ran away from the LORD and headed for Tarshish. He went down to Joppa, where he found a ship bound for that port. After paying the fare, he went aboard and sailed for Tarshish to flee from the LORD. Jonah 1:1-3**

I am just as guilty of this as anyone else! When we turn down opportunities, we are turning down God and the invitation to share His kingdom, His love, His mercy and His word with someone who might need it desperately. God wants to use us to bring others to His kingdom. I don't know about you, but I don't want to miss out on an opportunity like that from Him. It's what I live for – what we should live for every day. The good news is that it's not too late. It is never too late with God. Even if we turn away from Him, He will never turn away from us. Open your heart and mind to the will of God today, let Him pour into your life and He will seep out into all your actions.

**Then Jonah prayed to his God from the belly of the fish. He prayed: "In trouble, deep trouble, I prayed to God. He answered me. From the belly of the grave I cried, 'Help!' You heard my cry.**

You threw me into ocean's depths, into a watery grave, with ocean waves, ocean breakers crashing over me. I said, 'I've been thrown away, thrown out, out of your sight. I'll never again lay eyes on your Holy Temple.' Ocean gripped me by the throat. The ancient Abyss grabbed me and held tight. My head was all tangled in seaweed at the bottom of the sea where the mountains take root. I was as far down as a body can go, and the gates were slamming shut behind me forever— Yet you pulled me up from that grave alive, O God, my God! When my life was slipping away, I remembered God, and my prayer got through to you, made it all the way to your Holy Temple. Those who worship hollow gods, god-frauds, walk away from their only true love. But I'm worshiping you, God, calling out in thanksgiving! And I'll do what I promised I'd do! Salvation belongs to God!"
Jonah 2:1-9

~~~~~~

Monday – Find a word

Choose a word from the devotion or cited scriptures to reflect on for the week. Some examples: sovereign, righteous, almighty, full, uphold, future, hope, love, obedience. What is your word? _____

Search your Bible commentary. What verses use your word? List them here. Use your journal if you need additional space.

_____
_____
_____

Tuesday – Define

Choose one to two words to define and then reread the scriptures, replacing the word with the definition. How did it take your understanding to a new level?

Wednesday – Translate

Choose two or three different Bible translations. Read the Monday verses (cited in the devotional or found in your study) in each translation. Now write them in your journal.

Thursday – Go the Distance

Read the entire chapter of your favorite verse for the week.

Friday – Prayer

Close your eyes and talk to God or write out your prayer in your journal.

Your journey doesn't have to end here. Visit **www.godchickdevotions.com** to learn more about Allison, her books and upcoming speaking engagements. You can also subscribe to her blog and receive a new devotion weekly.

\*\*\*

*I pray that out of his glorious riches he may strengthen you with power through his Spirit in your inner being, so that Christ may dwell in your hearts through faith. And I pray that you, being rooted and established in love, may have power, together with all the saints, to grasp how wide and long and high and deep is the love of Christ, and to know this love that surpasses knowledge – that you may be filled to the measure of all the fullness of God. Now to him who is able to do immeasurably more than all we ask or imagine, according to his power that is at work within us, to him be glory in the church and in Christ Jesus throughout all generations, forever and ever! Amen. Ephesians 3:16-21*

## Why GodChick?

Many people have asked how I came up with "GodChick". So, I thought I would share the story behind the name.

About 4 years and 3 houses ago, my husband gave me a bracelet with "GodChick" inscribed on it. I, of course, LOVED it and wore it until the tarnish took over (it was only a $7 bracelet). Once I had to retire the bracelet to my jewelry box, I started to think about what I could do to keep it a part of me. I searched the North Carolina Division of Motor Vehicles database and found that no one in NC had "GodChick" as their license tag. I scooped it up.

Keep in mind, this is way before God had begun my ministry. This was also during the time that we had a Ralph Waldo Emerson's quote "Let us be silent so that we may hear the whisper of God" above our bath tub.

Nearly a year later, I started to blog what had only been a journal in a Word document. What better name than *The Whisper of God*. As God continued to grow the blog into a devotional and then a ministry it was clear that my website had to be godchickdevotions.com. I was, after all, the "GodChick" driving around town.

So it isn't anything earth shattering, but just another great story about how God weaves our lives together to accomplish His plan.

## Acknowledgements

To Mary Edna, Kelly and Debbie, thank you for your time, encouragement, opening your hearts and your homes. I always tell people how important it is to have friends who love you, pray for you and hold you accountable. Thank you for being those people in my life.

To my amazing Mom and Dad (a.k.a. Nonnie & Pop-Pop), I feel so blessed to be able to say, "I have the best parents in the world!" Thank you for loving me, giving me a foundation in Christ, logging a zillion hours of prayers on my behalf and for staying together all these years. I love you!!!

To Christie Love and many other Christian writers and leaders, thank you for inspiring me to pursue this ministry to encourage other women.

To my husband and children, I adore you and appreciate all the opportunities you give me, through actions, words and situations, to see God in the ordinary.

To the Newmiller Family, your faith, grace and perseverance through the toughest trial imaginable has been an inspiration to me and countless others.

To Jeannie, without you dear friend, this book would have so many typos and stray words it would be useless and never have the opportunity to touch the hearts of others. Thank you for generously sharing your abilities and time for this book.

To my Heavenly Father, YOU ROCK! I don't know what is coming next, but as my dear friend Jean said, "Life is so full and exciting if we will only believe!"